John Allen

Man, money and the Bible

Biblical economics

John Allen

Man, money and the Bible
Biblical economics

ISBN/EAN: 9783337147105

Printed in Europe, USA, Canada, Australia, Japan

Cover: Foto ©Lupo / pixelio.de

More available books at **www.hansebooks.com**

MAN, MONEY, AND THE BIBLE;

OR,

BIBLICAL ECONOMICS.

A TREATISE UPON THE ECONOMICAL SYSTEM OF THE BIBLE,
AND ITS SOLUTION OF THE SOCIAL PROBLEMS THAT
CONFRONT THE NINETEENTH CENTURY.

———

BY REV. JOHN R. ALLEN, D.D.

———

PRINTED FOR THE AUTHOR.
PUBLISHING HOUSE OF THE METHODIST EPISCOPAL CHURCH, SOUTH.
BARBEE & SMITH, AGENTS, NASHVILLE, TENN.
1891.

Entered, according to Act of Congress, in the year 1891,
BY JOHN R. ALLEN,
In the Office of the Librarian of Congress, at Washington.

DEDICATION.

TO

Mrs. M. A. Allen,

The Mother Who Aided My Childhood,

AND TO

Mrs. Mollie Allen,

The Wife Who Has Cheered My Manhood, as a Slight Mark of the Respect and Affection He Cherishes for Them,

THIS BOOK IS DEDICATED BY

The Author.

PREFACE.

In this monograph I have endeavored to show the practicability of constructing a system of economy from the principles of divine revelation, rather than to actually construct one. I do not believe that finite wisdom can discover the great fundamental laws of sociology without divine help. Ethics tried once to walk alone, but she proved so feeble that she was compelled to come back and lean reverently on the Word of God for support. I believe that political economy must do the same. In this work I try to show the wisdom of such a course. Man rebels against the position of mere learner to which this reduces him; he would much rather display his own wisdom in the construction of a system of economics than take a ready-made one from his Creator. But this humility will be good for him, and it is his only course.

It may be asked: "If this system is in the Bible, why not go direct to the Bible for it? Why write this book?" A recent writer has said that the Bible contains theology just as the heavens contain astronomy, but man must in each case search out the science from the *data* which God has given him. Just so these Scriptures contain anthropology, which contains sociology, which contains economics; but man is left to hunt out and classify these principles which God has revealed.

This is the task which I have set myself, and to which I have given time, labor, and prayer. If I have contributed any light at all upon this subject, which I believe to be the most important now up for discussion, I shall be rewarded for all my work. For years I have revolved these questions in my mind, and have labored upon these problems. The results are here; the value will soon be determined.

INTRODUCTION.

In our day the world of thought is in a ferment. The foundations of things are being dug up and examined as with a lighted torch. Past solutions of problems do not satisfy. Each man must find a solution for himself. The traditional and accepted order of things must be called before the bar of human judgment, and show cause why it should continue to be, and why it would not be right for it to give way to another and a better order.

Religion herself, the guide and comfort of man here, and the foundation for his hope hereafter, has been compelled to prove anew her right to fill her exalted offices. Out of that crucial ordeal of criticism she has come with added beauty and undiminished power, shorn only of some meretricious ornaments which man without divine warrant had added, in a vain and foolish effort to heighten her charms.

Among the things whose right to be is being examined in our day are the traditional and accepted customs of getting and holding property. A mass of human beings, crushed by these customs into hopeless poverty and suffering, are no longer disposed to submit as to an unalterable decree of fate, or as to a beneficent providence which will make up for the ills of their present state in a future world. They have seen the monarch called into the august court of humanity, and required to establish his claim to a divine right to rule; and they have seen judgment rendered against him. They have seen the aristocratic and intelligent classes summoned before the same bar, and required to make good their title to control the destinies of the race; and judgment went against them. Now the *sans callottes* are clamorous that the third estate, the wealth gatherers and holders, shall come into that great court and show cause why they should retain the special privileges which they have heretofore possessed. The defendants deny jurisdiction; but the papers have been served, and the trial will go on, *nolens volens*, to what end God only knows. Questions have been raised in the meantime which must be answered; they press for answer. The right to land, the title to all property, the rights of inheritance and bequest, the power to employ and discharge, the right to combine—both in regard to capital and labor—to strike and boycott; all these are up for discussion, and the diverse and jangling voices attempting an answer make a pandemonium. Meantime numbers of human beings suffer—not in silence or patience, but with wild outcries or in sullen anger that bodes no good.

Is not there a science devoted to the answer of all these economic questions? and have not the foremost of intellects laid down its principles in clear and truth-seeming *formulæ?* Let the crowd hush, and hear their philosophic answer to these problems. But the crowd will not hush; because those answers feed not the hungry, nor clothe the naked, nor warm the freezing. In fact, the mightiest voices among these *savants* say, coldly and calmly, that it is better for some to starve and others to freeze, as the survivors will be in better condition. Somehow the wretched victims cannot be reconciled to this sort of vicarious sacrifice, nor can the rest of mankind be made to pay much more respect to the deliverances of political economy. Upon this subject Henry George, the most potent voice America has yet produced in economic science, speaks as follows: "That political economy, as at present taught, does not explain the persistency of poverty amid advancing wealth, in a manner which accords with the deep-seated perceptions of men; that the unquestionable truths which it does teach are unrelated and disjointed; that it has failed to make the progress in popular thought that truth, even when unpleasant, must make; that, on the contrary, after a century of cultivation, during which it has engrossed the attention of some of the most subtle and powerful intellects, it should be spurned by the statesman, scouted by the masses, and relegated, in the opinion of many educated and thinking men, to the rank of a pseudo-science in which nothing is fixed or can be fixed, must, it seems to me, be due not to any inability of the science when properly pursued, but to some false step in its premises or overlooked factor in its estimates."

Ah, that missing factor! Has George picked up the dropped stitch? So complex has our modern civilization become that it becomes exceedingly important that a few great principles of sociology be established, the observance of which will "make for

Introduction.

righteousness" and justice and for the material advancement of the people. But amid the warring interests of humanity what man is able to foresee the working of any new principle— whether, taken on the whole, it will be advantageous or disadvantageous? We need these new principles in economic science. Now if they are not already in existence, where shall we go to get them? They must be simple, obvious, axiomatic, and authoritative.

Is there a philosopher among us who is prepared to give them to us? If there were, is there any chance for his utterances to come with that authority which is demanded? I think either is beyond hope. There are too many factors entering into the simplest problem of sociology for any mind occupying no higher plane than the human intellect to ever arrive at a correct solution.

But it may be said that it is not new principles which are wanted, but simply the discovery of the principles or laws of sociology which have acted for good in the past, and laying them down for man's guidance in the future. Here indeed we are more capable of doing something, and in this field the great political economists have added much that is valuable to human thought, and have contributed their quota to the advancement of the race; but we confess that they seem to us to have been much more successful in pointing out the evil principles—the things which have caused friction and confusion, and hence are to be avoided—than in discovering beneficial laws. Some at least of the latter, of at least the Mills school of economists, appear to be actually pernicious. The very evils which are taking on such a threatening character in our day are the legitimate outgrowth of these maxims of philosophers, which they have stated as dogmatically as if they were axiomatic. Have they not taught us that selfishness is, and ought to be, the controlling principle with man? Have they not taught that vice and crime and starvation and debauchery and war and pestilence are good things, as they either prevent the addition to a dense population or thin it out?

Let us test, as a means of determining the value of the axioms of this science, what Henry George calls their basis: "For political economy is not a set of dogmas. It is the science which, in the sequence of certain phenomena, seeks to trace mutual relations and to identify cause and effect, just as the physical sciences seek to do in other sets of phenomena. It lays its foundations upon firm ground. The premises from which it makes its deductions are truths which have the highest sanctions, axioms which we all recognize, upon which we safely base the reasonings and actions of every-day life, and which may be reduced to the metaphysical expression of the physical law that motion seeks the line of least resistance—viz., that men seek to gratify their desires with the least exertion. Proceeding from a basis thus assured, its processes, which consist simply in identification and separation, have the same certainty. In this sense it is as exact a science as geometry, which from similar truths relative to space obtains its conclusions by similar means, and its conclusions when valid should be as self-apparent. And although in the domain of political economy we cannot test our theories by artificially produced combinations or conditions, as may be done in some of the other sciences; yet we can apply tests no less conclusive by comparing societies in which different conditions exist, or by in imagination separating, combining, adding, or eliminating forces or factors of known direction."

Here, then, it is: "Men seek to gratify their desires with the least exertion. In this sense it is as exact a science as geometry." Let us test this exactitude: "Men seek to gratify their desires." Now if there were any uniformity in men's desires, we might have a basis for a science; but some men desire present gratification, some financial or business success, some indolent ease, some scholastic attainments, some literary fame, some to grasp the reins of power, some virtue, holiness, purity. Their desires are not only not uniform, but they lie in entirely different planes—the plane of the sensuous, the intellectual, the moral. If Henry George be correct in his statement, how can the science be worth any thing which starts with an assumption of uniformity where there is the utmost possible divergence?

It may be said that the law remains the same, however diverse the objects of desire. True, but we must have knowledge of the things desired before we can calculate the results this law will work out. Hence there must be absolute uniformity in the character of humanity's desires, or there must be an exact knowledge of the amount and character of the divergence, or

Introduction. 11

your science will not only be inexact, but false. Who cannot see at a glance that there are too many unknown and unknowable factors here for any thing like a foundation for a science? The truth is that such an effort to make an exact science is consciously or unconsciously the outgrowth of a belief that man is a thing, and not a power; and hence that his actions in given circumstances may be calculated as we calculate the eclipse of the sun. Surely it is not necessary for me to refute this assumption here. If it were true, then such men as William of Orange, George Washington, Livingston, Peabody, Howard, and all the names who have uplifted humanity and advanced the interests of the race by self-sacrifice, would be impossible. History would be a monotonous record of Cæsars, Napoleons, Goulds, Fisks, *et id omne genus.* Here is the mistake of the political economists of the Mill school. They have assumed not only that most men are selfish, but that all men are and ought to be, and that wealth is and ought to be the object of their desires. It is true that they have pointed out and condemned some policies that are eminently grounded in narrow selfishness; but they do it by proving that such or such a policy is a mistaken effort to build up self not because it is wrong, but because it fails to accomplish its object. And they simply propose to furnish misguided selfishness with a better pilot.

That, starting with this error, the science has come so near explaining the events of the past and disclosing the motive power behind some of the most complex movements of the present, that in practical life it has been nearly approximately true, comes from the fact that there is so small an exception in the race to the rule laid down that men are selfish, and that the object of their desires is wealth. But it is the excepted fraction, small as it is numerically, which has exercised the greatest influence for good in the past; and the hope of the future lies in the increase of this fraction, and not in its elimination.

That school of the science of wealth which is here combated has assumed from the start that it was dealing with practical life, with men as they are; that it was its duty to tell them how they must act in order to secure advantage to themselves, and not how they ought to act to fulfill the measure of their obligation. But if there is any field for ethics—the science of right action—in this world, by what sort of logic can ethics be excluded from that part of a man's life which concerns the acquiring, holding, and managing of his wealth? Economics is in truth but a part of the wider and higher science of ethics, and the laws of right action which are discovered in this higher field are operative in this part of it. No man has ever had the right to banish "ought" and substitute "may" or "must" or "can" in this or any other department of human action. Economics, then, is simply a department of ethics.

There was an effort made in the last century to disassociate ethics or moral philosophy from religion, and make it stand alone. For awhile the effort seemed successful, but soon over all Europe the pernicious effect of this philosophy appeared in the growing immorality of the people. Coleridge and others entered the field to protest against the unnatural divorce of religion from morals, and to show that the life of the latter was derived from the former; nor have their arguments ever been answered. Man has never yet constructed a system of morals that did not derive its principles from religion, and did not look to religion for its sanctions. The revelation of God, as found in the Bible, is the foundation, not indeed for all the books written upon the subject of morality, but of all the recognized authority for moral action among the masses in civilized nations. This is a living, operative power among men. The cold abstractions of any philosopher, so far as they are independent of it, are powerless inanities.

Now then we see that religion is inclusive of ethics, and ethics is inclusive of economics; hence economics is included in religion, and inseparable from it. If we go to religion—the real science of sociology, including what man ought to be in himself, and how he ought to act toward all others—we find there for economics, as for the whole field of ethics, the simple principles which we need. They have, too, all the desirable qualities—simplicity and obviousness, that all may understand; they are axiomatic, commanding the immediate assent of men's minds; they are authoritative, resting upon God's own word.

These principles, however, are not accepted and acted upon by a majority of the people; but only by a small minority. These principles, worked out, give us a system of economics as it ought to be, and not as it actually is. Yet it is true that that fraction in whose development the future of the world depends

Introduction. 13

are all found here; and more or less they, consciously or unconsciously, believe in and practice these Christian principles.

Mr. Mill gives us the actual econonomic principles upon which the majority of men act, but he makes a grievous error in not calculating the variation from the selfish principle on the part of those who are guided in their actions by higher motives than this. By just so much he makes an erroneous science. Then, too, he makes a mistake in accepting the motives which ordinarily move men as right, and to be encouraged. Many of these natural motives are wrong, and man can only advance as they are eliminated.

But if we do not construct the science of economics upon and from this principle of selfishness—not well-regulated self-love—then there is only one other way to construct a logical treatise, and that is to construct it upon and from the great precepts of the Bible. Good books about economics may be written, containing much truth, but they cannot be logical or consistent unless they proceed from one or the other of these centers; and to be correct they must in either case take into consideration the existence of the contrary principle with which it is at war, and which acts as a brake upon the perfect operation of the principle which may be in hand.

In this little book, when I combat political economy, it is the selfish school of which I am speaking. I shall try here to hunt out and show the correlation of these economic principles of the Bible; and to show that they are practical, sensible, and operate to the best interest of the individual and of the body politic.

I believe that the true relation of the wealth-getter to society, either upon a small or a large scale, and his duty, have never been rightly presented.

The class of philosophers whom we oppose have calmly waved religion out of the realm of practical business. I hear Adam Smith: "The institutions for the instruction of men of all ages are chiefly those for religious instruction. This is a species of instruction of which the object is not so much to render the people good citizens in this world as to prepare them for another and better world in the life to come."

Nor are these philosophers alone responsible for this idea of the separateness of practical business and religion. The Church has taught little else in reference to wealth-getting than that it was wrong. Here is what John Wesley says on the subject:

"Therefore 'lay not up for yourselves treasures upon earth, where moth and rust doth corrupt, and where thieves break through and steal.' If you do, it is plain your eye is evil; it is not singly fixed on God. With regard to most of the commandments of God, whether relating to the heart or life, the heathens of Africa or America stand much on a level with those that are called Christians. The Christians observe them (a few only being excepted) very near as much as the heathens. For instance, the generality of the natives of England, commonly called Christians, are as sober and as temperate as the generality of the heathens near the Cape of Good Hope. And so the Dutch or French Christians are as humble and as chaste as the Choctaw or Cherokee Indians. It is not easy to say, when we compare the bulk of the nations in Europe with those in America, whether the superiority lies on the one side or the other. At least, the American has not much the advantage. But we cannot affirm this with regard to the command now before us. Here the heathen has far the pre-eminence. He desires and seeks nothing more than plain food to eat and plain raiment to put on, and he seeks this only from day to day. He reserves, he lays up nothing, unless it be as much corn at one season of the year as he will need before that season returns. This command, therefore, the heathens, though they know it not, do constantly and punctually observe. They 'lay up for themselves no treasures upon earth,' no stores of purple or fine linen, of gold or silver, which either 'moth or rust may corrupt, or thieves break through and steal.' But how do the Christians observe what they profess to receive as a command of the most high God? Not at all; not in any degree; no more than if no such command had ever been given to man. Even the good Christians, as they are accounted by others as well as themselves, pay no manner of regard thereto. It might as well be still hid in its original Greek, for any notice they take of it. In what Christian city do you find one man of five hundred who makes the least scruple of laying up just as much treasure as he can, of increasing his goods just as far as he is able? There are, indeed, those who would not do this unjustly; there are many who will neither rob nor steal, and some who will not defraud their neighbor—nay, who will not gain either by his ignorance or necessity.

"But this is quite another point. Even these do not scruple the thing, but the manner of it. They do not scruple the 'laying up treasures upon earth,' but the laying them up by dishonesty. They do not start at disobeying Christ, but at a breach of heathen morality; so that even these honest men do no more obey this command than a highwayman or a house-breaker. Nay, they never designed to obey it. From their youth up it never entered into their thoughts. They were bred up by their Christian parents, masters, and friends, without any instruction at all concerning it, unless it were this: to break it as soon and as much as they could, and to continue breaking it to their lives' end." ("Wesley's Sermons," Vol. II., p. 13.)

Wesley recognizes the inclusion of economics in religion:

"From those which are commonly termed religious actions, and which are real branches of true religion where they spring from a pure and holy intention, and are performed in a manner suitable thereto, our Lord proceeds to the actions of common life, and shows that the same purity of intention is as indispensably required in our ordinary business as in giving alms or fasting or prayer.

"And without question the same purity of intention which makes our alms and devotions acceptable must also make our labor or employment a proper offering to God. If a man pursues his business that he may raise himself to a state of figure and riches in the world, he is no longer serving God in his employment, and has no more title to a reward from God than he who gives alms that he may be seen or prays that he may be heard of men; for vain and earthly designs are no more allowable in our employments than in our alms and devotions. They are not only evil when they mix with our good works [with our religious actions], but they have the same evil nature when they enter into the common business of our employments. If it were allowable to pursue them in our worldly employments, it would be allowable to pursue them in our devotions. But as our alms and devotions are not an acceptable service but when they proceed from a pure intention, so our common employment cannot be reckoned a service to him but when it is performed with the same piety of heart." ("Wesley's Sermons," Vol. II., p. 7.)

But the following extract shows that religion allowed, in Mr. Wesley's estimation, wealth-getting to go only to the provision for the simplest necessaries of life:

"Do you ask what it is to 'lay up treasures on earth?' It will be needful to examine this thoroughly. And let us first observe what is not forbidden in this command, that we may then clearly discern what is.

"We are not forbidden in this command, first, to 'provide things honest in the sight of all men,' to provide wherewith we may render unto all their due, whatsoever they can justly demand of us. So far from it that we are taught of God to 'owe no man any thing.' We ought, therefore, to use all diligence in our calling in order to owe no man any thing; this being no other than a plain law of common justice, which our Lord came 'not to destroy, but to fulfill.'

"Neither, secondly, does he here forbid the providing for ourselves such things as are needful for the body—a sufficiency of plain, wholesome food to eat and clean raiment to put on. Yea, it is our duty, so far as God puts it into our power, to provide these things also, to the end that we may eat our own bread and be burdensome to no man.

"Nor yet are we forbidden, thirdly, to provide for our children and for those of our own household. This also it is our duty to do, even upon principles of heathen morality. Every man ought to provide the plain necessaries of life, both for his own wife and children, and to put them in a capacity of providing these for themselves when he has gone hence and is no more seen. I say of providing these, the plain necessaries of life—not delicacies, not superfluities—and that by their diligent labor; for it is no man's duty to furnish them, any more than himself, with the means either for luxury or idleness. But if any man provide not thus far for his own children (as well as for the widows of his own house, of whom primarily St. Paul is speaking in those well-known words to Timothy), he hath practically 'denied the faith,' and is 'worse than an infidel' or heathen.

"Lastly, we are not forbidden in these words to lay up, from time to time, what is needful for the carrying on of our worldly business in such a measure and degree as is sufficient to answer the foregoing purposes in such a measure as, first, to owe no man any thing; secondly, to procure for ourselves the necessaries of life; and, thirdly, to furnish those of our own house with them while we live, and with the means of procuring them when we are gone to God.

"We may now clearly discern (unless we are unwilling to discern it) what that is which is forbidden here. It is the designedly procuring more of this world's goods than will answer the foregoing purposes. The laboring after a larger measure of worldly substance, a larger increase of gold and silver, the laying up any more than these ends require, is what is here expressly and absolutely forbidden. If the words have any meaning at all, it must be this; for they are capable of no other. Consequently whoever he is that, owing no man any thing, and having food and raiment for himself and his household, together with a sufficiency to carry on his worldly business, so far as answers these reasonable purposes; whosoever, I say, being already in these circumstances, seeks a still larger portion on earth, he lives in an open, habitual denial of the Lord that bought him. 'He hath [practically] denied the faith, and is worse than [an African or American] infidel.'"

Mr. Wesley here represents the very best and strongest of Christian teaching in the past; and a careful study of his words shows that a man's right action, in his opinion, is reduced to getting a living.

Now I go so far as to say, as over against Mr. Adam Smith on the one hand, that the great object of religious instruction is, first, to make a man a good citizen of this world, that he may be fit for citizenship in a better; and over against Mr. Wesley, on the other hand, that it may be a man's duty to accumulate large wealth. There is no more reason for pressing the words of the text Mr. Wesley stresses so strongly as an absolute command against accumulation than there is for saying that Christ commands us to hate our parents when he says: "He that hateth not father and mother is not worthy of me." He bids us pay attention to the heavenly rather than the earthly, to make the soul of more importance than the body; and he does forbid laying up purely from selfish motives.

Religion has largely repudiated the wealth-getter in her teachings, if not in her practice; and as a natural consequence the man who felt within himself the God-implanted gifts of an *entrepreneur* (a manager of affairs) and yet taught that to go into his mighty projects for money-making was a sin, either repudiated his Christianity or repressed and suppressed his natural talent. Hence there has been a divorce between these two things to their mutual injury, and to the great misfortune of the human race. Religion and the race need the wealth-getter, and the wealth-getter may be the most religious of men, not necessarily by stripping himself of his wealth, but by simply using it as the Bible requires.

Does not the Saviour say: "How hardly shall they that have riches enter into the kingdom of God?" To be sure, and he says: "The things that are impossible with men are possible with God." This hard thing is not only possible with God, but in his word he has revealed how it can be accomplished by men. All wealth accumulated contrary to the laws he has laid down and all wealth held contrary to them is sin, and that without regard to the amount; and wealth secured and held in accord with the divine law is evidence of the highest virtue.

I believe that great harm has been done in the realm of economics by following the rush-light of infidel writers instead of the sunlight of the word of God. I believe that the laws of revelation are as true, as authoritative, as beneficial here as in any other part of man's work. Hence in this work I am simply trying to hunt out these laws of the Bible, and to show their relations. I assume an acquaintance with the ordinary works of political economy, and only treat the subject so far as the truths of the Bible bear upon it. It is not a political economy, but a Biblical economics, dealing mostly with the individual, and but little with the body politic.

It may be objected that this effort to bring economics under the laws of the Bible is going in the direction of mediævalism, subjecting a science to religious tests. I answer: Material sciences are not the subjects of revelation, and are not to be tested by it; but the very content of revelation is men's duty to God and each other. Here it must be true, or it stands discredited and disproved. Into this realm political economy intrudes, and it must be judged by the Bible, or we must throw the Bible away.

The larger portion of Part I. is devoted to showing the logical consequences of some of the principles generally accepted by political economists. I simply accept these and their consequences for a time, and eventually substitute the principles of

Introduction. 19

the kingdom of Christ for them. I will here say, that the reader may at all times have the key to my position, that I believe Socialism or Christianity—one or the other—is true. They are mutually exclusive, and they exclude all other hypotheses. This book is intended to show that the principles of Christianity are alone the right ones.

CONTENTS.

PART I.
A Discussion of Property and the Title by Which It Is Held.

CHAPTER I. PAGE
The Title to Property in General, and to Land Especially, Investigated 25

CHAPTER II.
An Investigation of the Title Derived by Inheritance and Bequest.. 33

CHAPTER III.
An Investigation of Titles Derived from Sharp Practices, Combines, Stock-watering, Trusts, etc.—Conclusions from Premises 40

CHAPTER IV.
The Absolute Title to Property Is in God—Man Derives His Title from God.................................... 44

CHAPTER V.
The Method of the Transfer of Property to the Individual Man, and the Character of Title He Receives.......... 50

PART II.
Biblical Economics Proper.

CHAPTER I.
Man Must Recognize His Stewardship.................... 59

CHAPTER II.
Love Thy Neighbor as Thyself......................... 68

CHAPTER III.
Mutual Consideration, Mutual Helpfulness, and Doing All Work as unto God..................................... 77

Chapter IV.
Discontent and Love of Money Condemned. 84

Chapter V.
Delay of Payments to Laborers, Stealing, Unforgiveness, and Sabbath-breaking Forbidden..................... 92

Chapter VI.
Some Absolute Sociological Laws....................... 95

PART III.
What Revolution Shall It Be?

Chapter I.
Revolution Imminent 109

Chapter II.
Revolution Proposed in Co-operation.................... 115

Chapter III.
The Revolution Proposed by Henry George in Land Ownership.. 120

Chapter IV.
The Revolution Proposed in Socialism................... 127

Chapter V.
Christianity or Socialism 133

PART IV.
What Can We Do To Promote Reformation in Money Matters?

Chapter I.
What Can Individuals Do?............................. 147

Chapter II.
What Can and Should the State Do?.................... 158

Chapter III.
What Can and Ought the Church to Do?................ 173

PART I.

A DISCUSSION OF PROPERTY AND THE TITLE BY WHICH IT IS HELD.

MAN, MONEY, AND THE BIBLE.

CHAPTER I.

THE TITLE TO PROPERTY IN GENERAL, AND TO LAND ESPECIALLY, INVESTIGATED.

IN prosecuting our inquiry, it is necessary for us to investigate the title by which man holds his property. The question is: Why is it his? What right has he to it more than another?

"It is his because he made it or bought it," would be the common answer. The first part of this answer may be accepted as correct: *What a man makes is his.* But buying by no means always gives a good title. The man from whom a party buys must have a good title, and the man from whom the second party bought, and the man from whom the third party bought; and so on, back to the original maker. If the title at the start was bad, then no subsequent number of transfers can correct it. For instance, a chair-maker makes a chair. It is his, and he can sell it, and the title of the man buying it will be as good as his own; and so with all transfers that can be traced back to him. Suppose, however, that some one should steal the chair from the maker. Then the thief, of course, has no title; and hence the man who buys from him can get no title, although he may pay the full value of the article; nor could a hundred transfers, starting from this bad source, make the title good. The maker of the chair, who has been unjustly deprived of it, can in equity reclaim it wherever he may find it.

Very little of what any of us possess has been made by ourselves; most of it has been bought. Now, did we buy a good title? Perhaps if the chain of title were traced back to its original source, it would be found to have started in fraud. If so, then our title is clouded.

Starting, then, with the two principles—What a man makes is his, and *Transfer cannot improve a bad title*—we will investigate the right to the various kinds of property held by man.

The validity of all our titles to land has long been raised by political economists of high standing. Henry George is by no means the oldest or the foremost philosopher who has questioned this title. Hear what John Stuart Mill says: "These are the reasons which form the justification, in an economical point of view, of property in land. It is seen that they are only valid in so far as the proprietor of land is its improver. Whenever, in any country, the proprietor, generally speaking, ceases to be the improver, political economy has nothing to say in defense of landed property, as there established. In no sound theory of private property was it ever contemplated that the proprietor of land should be merely a sinecurist quartered on it." (Book II., Chap. II., § 6.)

This sweeps away all real title to unimproved lands, whether wild lands or unimproved lots in a city. In fact, it denies title to land, and recognizes it only in the improvements upon the land. To this logical end his disciple, Henry George, has gone; and he presents his views with decided force. Of this, however, we will give the reader an opportunity of judging by an extended extract:

And for this reason, that which a man makes or produces is his own, as against all the world—to enjoy or to destroy, to use, to exchange, or to give. No one else can rightfully claim it, and his exclusive right to it involves no wrong to any one else. Thus there is to every thing produced by human exertion a clear and indisputable title to exclusive possession and enjoyment, which is perfectly consistent with justice, as it descends from the original producer, in whom it vested by natural law. The pen with which I am writing is justly mine. No other human being can rightly lay claim to it, for in me is the title of the producers who made it. It has become mine, because transferred to me by the stationer, to whom it was transferred by the importer, who obtained the exclusive right to it by transfer from the manufacturer; in whom, by the same process of purchase, vested the rights of those who dug the material from the ground and shaped it into a pen. Thus my exclusive right of ownership in the pen springs from the natural right of the individual to the use of his own faculties.

Now this is not only the original source from which all ideas of exclusive ownership arise—as is evident from the natural tendency of the mind to revert to it when the idea of exclusive ownership is questioned, and the manner in which social relations develop—but it is necessarily the only source. There can be to the ownership of any thing no rightful title which is not derived from the title of the producer and does not rest upon the natural right of the man to himself. There can be no other rightful title; because (1) there is no other natural right from which any other title can be derived; and (2) because the recognition of any other title is inconsistent with and destructive of this.

1. For what other right exists from which the right to the exclusive possession of any thing can be derived, save the right of a man to himself? With what other power is man by nature clothed, save the power of exerting his own faculties? How can he in any other way act upon or affect material things or other men? Paralyze the motor nerves, and your man has no more external influence or power than a log or a stone. From what else, then, can the right of possessing and controlling things be derived?

If it springs not from man himself, from what can it spring? Nature acknowledges no ownership or control in man, save as the result of exertion. In no other way can her treasures be drawn forth, her powers directed, or her forces utilized or controlled. She makes no discriminations among men, but is to all absolutely impartial. She knows no distinction between master and slave, king and subject, saint and sinner. All men to her stand upon an equal footing and have equal rights. She recognizes no claim but that of labor, and recognizes that without respect to the claimant. If a pirate spread his sails, the wind will fill them as well as it will fill those of a peaceful merchantman or missionary bark; if a king and a common man be thrown overboard, neither can keep his head above water except by swimming; birds will not come to be shot by the proprietor of the soil any quicker than they will come to be shot by the poacher; fish will bite or will not bite at a hook in utter disregard of whether it is offered them by a good little boy who goes to Sunday-school or a bad little boy who plays truant; grain will grow only as the ground is prepared and the seed sown; it is only at the call of labor that ore can be raised from the mine; the sun shines and the rain falls alike upon the just and the unjust. The laws of nature are decrees of the Creator. There is written in them no recognition of any right save that of labor; and in them is written broadly and clearly the equal right of all men to the use and enjoyment of nature: to apply to her by their exertions, and to receive and possess her reward. Hence, as nature gives only to labor, the exertion of labor in production is the only title to exclusive possession.

2. This right of ownership that springs from labor excludes the possibility of any other right of ownership. If a man be rightfully entitled to the produce of his labor, then no one can be rightfully entitled to the ownership of any thing which is not the produce of his labor, or the labor of some one else from whom the right has passed to him. If production gives to the producer the right to exclusive possession and enjoyment, there can rightfully be no exclusive possession and enjoyment of any thing not the production of labor, and the recognition of private property in land is a wrong; for the right to the produce of labor cannot be enjoyed without the right to the free use of the opportunities offered by nature, and to admit the right of prop-

erty in these is to deny the right of property in the produce of labor. When non-producers can claim as rent a portion of the wealth created by producers, the right of producers to the fruits of their labor is to that extent denied.

There is no escape from this position. To affirm that a man can rightfully claim exclusive ownership in his own labor when embodied in material things is to deny that any one can rightfully claim exclusive ownership in land. To affirm the rightfulness of property in land is to affirm a claim which has no warrant in nature, as against a claim founded in the organization of man and the laws of the material universe.

What most prevents the realization of the injustice of private property in land is the habit of including all the things that are made the subject of ownership, in one category, as property; or, if any distinction is made, drawing the line, according to the unphilosophical distinction of the lawyers, between personal property and real estate, or things movable and things immovable. The real and natural distinction is between things which are the produce of labor and things which are the gratuitous offerings of nature; or, to adopt the terms of political economy, between wealth and land.

These two classes of things are in essence and relations widely different, and to class them together as property is to confuse all thought when we come to consider the justice and injustice, the right or the wrong of property.

A house and the lot on which it stands are alike property, as being the subject of ownership, and are alike classed by the lawyers as real estate. Yet in nature and relations they differ widely. The one is produced by human labor, and belongs to the class in political economy styled wealth. The other is a part of nature, and belongs to the class in political economy styled land. The essential character of one class of things is that they embody labor, are brought into being by human exertion—their existence or non-existence, their increase or diminution depending on man. The essential character of the other class of things is that they do not embody labor, and exist irrespective of human exertion and irrespective of man. They are the field or environment in which man finds himself, the store-house from which his needs must be supplied, the raw material upon which and the forces with which alone his labor can act.

The moment this distinction is realized, that moment is it seen that the sanction which natural justice gives to one species of property is denied to the other; that the rightfulness which attaches to individual property in the produce of labor implies the wrongfulness of individual property in land; that, whereas the recognition of the one places all men upon equal terms, securing to each the due reward of his labor, the recognition of the other is the denial of the equal rights of men, permitting those who do not labor to take the natural reward of those who do. . . . The equal right of all men to the use of land is as clear as their equal right to breathe the air. It is a right proclaimed by the fact of their existence; for we cannot suppose that some men have the right to be in this world, and others no right.

If we are all here by the equal permission of the Creator, we are all here with an equal title to the enjoyment of his bounty, with an equal right to the use of all that nature so impartially offers. This is a right that is natural and inalienable; it is a right that invests in every human being as he enters the world, and which during his continuance in the world can only be limited by the equal rights of others. There is in nature no such thing as a fee simple in land. There is on earth no power which can rightfully make a grant of exclusive ownership in land. If all existing men were to unite to grant away their equal rights, they could not grant away the rights of those who follow them; for what are we but tenants for a day? Have we made the earth, that we should determine the rights of those who after us shall tenant it in their turn? The Almighty, who created the earth for man and man for the earth, has entailed it upon all the generations of the children of men by a decree written upon the constitution of all things—a decree which no human action can bar and no prescription determine. Let the parchments be ever so many, or possession ever so long, natural justice can recognize no right in one man to the possession and enjoyment of land that is not equally the right of all his fellows. Though his titles have been acquiesced in by generation after generation, to the landed estates of the Duke of Westminster the poorest child that is born in London to-day has as much right as has his eldest son. Though the sovereign people of the State of New York consent to the landed possessions of the Astors, the puniest infant that comes wailing into the world, in the squalidest room of the most miserable tenement house, becomes at that moment seized of an equal right with the millionaires; and it is robbed if the right is denied. . . . As for the deduction of a complete and exclusive individual right to land from priority of occupation, that is, if possible, the most absurd ground on which land ownership can be defended. Priority of occupation give exclusive and perpetual title to the surface of a globe on which, in the order of nature, countless generations succeed each other? Had the men of the last generation any better right to the use of this world than we of this, or the men of a hundred years ago, or of a thousand years ago? had the mound-builders or the cave-dwellers—the contemporaries of the mastodon and the three-toed horse—or the generations still farther back, who, in dim eons that we can only think of as geologic periods, followed each other on the earth we now tenant for our little day?

Has the first comer at a banquet the right to turn back all the chairs, and claim that none of the other guests shall partake of the food provided, except as they make terms with him? Does the first man who presents a ticket at the door of a theater and passes in acquire by his priority the right to shut the doors and have the performance go on for him alone? Does the first passenger who enters a railroad car obtain the right to scatter his baggage over all the seats and compel the passengers who come in after him to stand up?

The cases are perfectly analogous. We arrive and we depart, guests at a banquet continually spread, spectators and participants in an entertainment where yet there is room for all who come, passengers from station to station on an orb that whirls through space—our rights to take and possess cannot be exclusive; they must be bounded everywhere by the equal rights of others. Just as the passenger in a railroad car may spread himself and his baggage over as many seats as he pleases until other passengers come in, so may a settler take and use as much land as he chooses until it is needed by others—a fact which is shown by the land acquiring a value—when his right must be curtailed by the equal rights of the others, and no priority of appropriation can give a right which will bar these equal rights of others. If this were not the case, then by priority of appropriation one man could acquire and could transmit to whom he pleased not merely the exclusive right to 160 acres, or to 640 acres, but to a whole township, a whole State, a whole continent. And to this manifest absurdity does the recognition of individual right to land come when carried to its ultimates—that any one human being, could he concentrate in himself the individual right to the land of any country, could expel therefrom all the rest of its inhabitants; and, could he thus concentrate the individual rights to the whole surface of the globe, he alone of all the teeming population of the earth would have the right to live. ("Progress and Poverty," Book VII., Chap. I.)

For the present I think that we may set it down that Mr. George makes out his case, and put down as an accepted principle: There is no absolute right to individual ownership in land.

CHAPTER II.

An Investigation of the Title Derived by Inheritance and Bequest.

LET us apply the same character of reasoning which Mr. George has used so forcibly to some other kind of property rights, and see if it does not destroy the title to other kinds of property besides that of land. Excuse reiteration in the discussion of the abstract right of property. It is necessary to have this point clear, and I wish you to see that I am proceeding according to the principles recognized in political economy.

Mr. George asks the question: "What is it that enables a man justly to say of a thing, 'It is mine?'" A correct answer to this question will give us the true title to property. Let us see some of the answers given. Mr. George says: "There can be to the ownership of any thing no rightful title which is not derived from the title of the producer, and does not rest upon the natural right of a man to himself." ("Progress and Poverty," p. 300.) Mr. Mill says: "Private property, in every defense made of it, is supposed to mean the guarantee to individuals of the fruit of their own labor and abstinence." ("Political Economy," Book II., Chap. I., § 3.) Also a careful definition in Book II., Chapter II., § 1: "The institution of property, when limited to its essential elements, consists in the recognition, in each person, of a right to the exclusive disposal of what he or she may have produced by their own exertions, or received—either by gift or fair agreement, without force or fraud—from those who produced it."

A man's title to any thing must rest on the fact that he produced it, or that he has purchased or received it as a gift from the one who made it, or that an unbroken chain of title stretches back, with no intervening fraud, to the maker.

Now what a man inherits cannot be reduced under any part of this definition. Where it comes as the result of bequest, it may be said to be a gift, of which we will speak directly; but where it is inherited as a result of the laws of descent, without having been willed, it cannot be said to be a gift. In this case is there any natural law of justice by which property can become a man's?

Any babe born helplessly into this world has a right to look for support until such time as it can take care of itself. The word "support" here means all that is necessary to its real well-being—including nurture, protection, education, and providing it a chance to make its own way. This claim every newborn one has primarily upon those who are responsible for its birth. If the parents have stored labor in the form we call wealth, then in the case of their death the child has a lien upon this wealth for this support. To this much of a parent's property the child has a natural and equitable right, whether the parent lives or dies, and without regard to the legitimacy or illegitimacy of its birth.

So much of property, then, as comes into a man's hands as the result of such a law as this, based in nature, is rightly his. Mill regards this in this light:

Whatever fortune a parent may have inherited, or, still more, may have acquired, I cannot admit that he owes to his children, merely because they are his children, to leave them rich, without the necessity of any exertion. I could not admit it, even if to be so left were always and certainly for the good of the children themselves. But this is in the highest degree uncertain. It depends on individual character. Without supposing extreme cases, it may be affirmed that in a majority of instances the good not only of society, but of the individuals, would be better consulted by bequeathing to them a moderate than a large provision. This, which is a common place of moralists—ancient and modern—is felt to be true by many intelligent parents, and would be acted upon much more frequently if they did not allow themselves to consider less what really is than what will be thought by others to be advantageous to the children. The duties of parents to their children are those which are indissolubly attached to the fact of causing existence of a human being. The parent owes to society to endeavor to make the child a good and valuable member of it; and owes to the children to provide, as far as depends on him, such education and such appliances and means as will enable them to start with a fair chance of achieving, by their own exertions, a successful life. To this every child has a claim, and I cannot admit that as a child he has a claim to more. There is a case in which these obligations present themselves in their true light, without any extrinsic circumstances to disguise or confuse them: it is that of an illegitimate child. ("Political Economy," Book II., § 3.)

Now if there is any argument from the basis of natural justice that recognizes any right to goods inherited, beyond this amount necessary to give a child a fair chance, and that construed liberally, I have never seen it.

The same argument which Mr. George has used so effectively, that man's exclusive right to what he has produced excludes the right of any man to what he has had no hand in producing, applies with just as much force to the wealth amassed by preceding generations as it does to the unearned values of nature or land.

The law which permits the disinheritance of heirs—even children—by will contravenes any thing like an inalienable right of inheritance. This law, setting aside the right of inheritance, recognizes the absolute right of man to will his possessions as he pleases.

Let us now investigate this right of bequest, and the title of all property held under it. Mr. Mill contends for this right:

> Nothing is implied in property but the right of each to his (or her) own faculties, to what can be produced by them, and to whatever he can get for them in a fair market; together with the right to give this to any other person if he chooses and the right of that other to receive and enjoy it. It follows, therefore, that although the right of bequest, or gift after death, forms part of the idea of private property, the right of inheritance, as distinguished from it, does not. ("Political Economy," Book II., Chap. II., § 3.)

It seems to me that the great logician has slipped here. Let us investigate this right to will property, taking the basis laid down for property—a man's right to himself and what he can make. A man makes or buys a good title to a piece of property. It is his while he lives—to enjoy, to use, to give away, or to destroy (the latter only true while reasoning from natural law, as according to the Bible and good morals he has no such right). He has gained a title to so much out of existing things. How long in time does that title extend? The right of bequest extends it beyond a man's life. He not only controls this property while living, but says who shall control it when he is dead. If a man's right to property extends an hour beyond his life, by what reasoning can it ever be terminated? Nature has set a limit to the time of man's acquisition and enjoyment of property; by what argument can unlimited right of control be defended?

There are two things entering into every product of values: man's work and the forces of nature. Let us suppose that A has by his own diligence and toil, intelligently directed, found a diamond; and that he hires B to cut and polish the stone for him, and pays him for his labor. There are three items entering into the value of that beautiful stone: First, the toil of A consumed in its discovery; second, the labor of B spent upon it, to which A now has a title by purchase; third, and in this case the principal item of value, the rarity and beauty of the stone, for which nature is to be thanked. Now all will admit A's right to enjoy this jewel, to sell it, or to give it away while he is living. But by the small amount of work relative to its value has he obtained a perpetual right to its control? I go so far as to say that if he can control it one hour after he has left this world for another, then there is no logical limit in time to its control.

Mr. Mill has the following discussion of the right of bequest:

Whether the power of bequest should itself be subject to limitation is an ulterior question of great importance. Unlike inheritance *ab intestato*, bequest is one of the attributes of property. The ownership of a thing cannot be looked upon as complete without the power of bestowing it, at death or during life, at the owner's pleasure; and all the reasons which recommend that private property should exist recommend *pro tanto* this extension of it. But property is only a means to an end, not itself the end.

Like an other proprietary rights, and even in a greater degree than most, the power of bequest may be so exercised as to conflict with the permanent interests of the human race. It does so when, not content with bequeathing an estate to A, the testator prescribes that on A's death it shall pass to his eldest son, and to that son's son, and so on forever. No doubt persons have occasionally exerted themselves more strenuously to acquire a fortune from a hope of founding a family in perpetuity; but the mischiefs to society of such perpetuities outweigh the value of this incentive to exertion; and the incentives in the case of those who have the opportunity of making large fortunes are strong enough without it. A similar abuse of the power of bequest is committed when a person who does the meritorious act of leaving property for public uses attempts to prescribe the details of its application in perpetuity; when, in founding a place of education, for instance, he dictates forever what doctrines shall be taught. It being impossible that any one should know what doctrines will be fit to be taught after he has been dead for centuries, the law ought not to give effect to such dispositions of property, unless subject to the perpetual revision, after a certain interval has elapsed, of a fitting authority. These are obvious limitations. ("Political Economy," Book II., Chap. II., § 4.)

Mr. Mill's argument that it would be contrary to public policy and the interests of society for the right of bequest to be perpetual is good and true; but is it not just as true that it is contrary to the interests of society for it to be at all? Great, massive fortunes are being piled up and enjoyed by individuals in our country, and then handed over by bequest to those who had no hand in gathering them. And these fortunes increase by their own inherit power of attraction, and in larger bulk go on to another generation. These heirs have not even the poor part of abstinence to their credit in the increase of their estates; for the income is simply more than they can spend, and yearly surplus swells the capital, already too large. This process can have no end so long as the unlimited right of bequest holds good. As a consequence, brainless, idle, and worthless people in many instances become the controllers of the destiny of vast numbers of our population, often crushing worthy laborers to obtain means to gratify their vices. Hence we have the same argument—the welfare of the body politic—for doing away entirely with the right of bequest that we have for limiting it.

Then to make a man's control end at the same time that nature has stepped in and taken it out of his hands is certainly the most logical time to terminate it. If his control goes beyond this dead line fixed in nature, then it goes on forever; and any interference is an injustice to a helpless dead man.

Reasoning, then, upon the natural basis laid down by the political economists, we conclude that there is good title to property derived by inheritance from parents to a limited amount (or by parents from children); but not otherwise. But title by bequest is worthless.

CHAPTER III.

An Investigation of Titles Derived from Sharp Practices, Combines, Stock-watering, Trusts, etc.—Conclusions from Premises.

A MAN has the exclusive right to what he has made or has derived by purchase from the maker. No one can take this property from him without giving an equivalent, and have any title to it, or be able to give any one else a title to it.

We can very readily see that one man of strong muscle has no right to force a weaker man to surrender his possessions to him. This is robbery, and robbery is one of the greatest of crimes. Nor does it change the character of the act if a weak man, by the aid of a fire-arm, intimidates a strong man and obtains his possessions. It is still robbery. Does it change the character of the act if a man of strong intellect outwits and befools a man of less mental power, and in that way obtains his possessions? Has the man any better right to use his mental superiority to overreach his neighbor than his muscular superiority to coerce him? None at all.

I do not mean that a man has no right to receive wages for mental work as well as for physical labor, but he must give an equivalent in mental work for the wages he receives. It may be instruction, help in business difficulty, mere entertainment, or he may invent some process or machine of value. He has a right to the results of the valuable thinking he has given to men. So, too, he has, as a tradesman or middle man of any character, a right to a reward for all the valuable work which he performs, and even for his skill in striking the public taste. But a man must give something for what he gets, to individuals or to the body politic.

Wherever, however, he renders no equivalent, but by some sort of scheming obtains wealth for himself from an individual, or from the public at large, he has no title in equity to that wealth, and he is incapable of transferring it with an equitable title. Such wealth belongs exactly to the category of our stolen chair. The title is tainted by fraud, and it can never be perfected by transfer.

This cuts off from good title all property obtained by corners on necessities, by stock-watering schemes, by trusts and combines, by gambling in margins, and all those ways which the fertile intellect of man has devised for getting something for nothing. Property so obtained does not belong by right to those who hold it, but the title has in reality never passed from those who were cheated out of it.

This is of course true of the more palpable frauds—such as lotteries, dishonest banks, malfeasances, and betrayals of trusts, and hundreds of adroit ways of stealing, which, though the public conscience may not condemn as forcibly as it does sneaking theft, yet they convey no better title than downright stealing.

Let us see how far these principles have carried us. You see we started from a basis which commends itself to common sense, and which has the approval of the foremost among political economists; and the reasoning will bear the tests of logic. Our conclusions, therefore, are all the more startling.

We have invalidated the title to all land. This includes all mining property, all timber, and all water power and wharfage property. It also includes all of the general mass of wealth which is the result of the past rents on land, to which the landlords, having no right, could get and give no real title. We have invalidated all individual title to the wealth accumulated by past generations, except that small part of their parents' estates to which children have a legitimate claim. Put these two things together—the invalidation of title to land and to property derived from inheritance and bequest—and we have the mass of real estate, including both land and improvements, among the things to which the individual can have no right. This is especially true in old countries, where the great part of the buildings were erected long ago. Then come in the deductions of the present chapter, sweeping away a large per cent. of the titles by which stocks, bonds, and personal property generally are held.

Now revert to the principle that transfer cannot cure a bad title, and try to calculate how much of the general mass of wealth about us has been at some time tainted by one or the other of these principles which have been adduced. Who can say that he has a clear title to any thing which he has not actually made himself? What wonder that there are men who believe that private property is public robbery? What wonder that there are those who believe not only in the logic which we have here employed, but believe with the force and zeal of fanatics in the conclusions to which this reasoning leads? Socialism has the same basis as received political economy; its conclusions are logical, are irrefragible, so far as they attack the title to the mass of property. Strip the writers of these strange and revolutionary doctrines, of their fiery rhetoric, of their intense hatred of Christianity, of their bombast and fustian, and you have about the same conclusions set forth in this and the two preceding chapters.

There is nothing left for us, then, but to go over to them, revolutionary and destructive of all peace and prosperity and all progress as they seem to us; or to find some other basis for title to property than that which political economy has thus far recognized. If the right to property is resting upon an injustice, then private property is sooner or later doomed.

CHAPTER IV.

THE ABSOLUTE TITLE TO PROPERTY IS IN GOD— MAN DERIVES HIS TITLE FROM GOD.

THE principles of political economy, pressed to their legitimate conclusions, teach, as we have seen, that man has no absolute or exclusive right to any property which has not been earned by himself, or given to him by some living one having a clear title, or derived by inheritance from the estate of his parents. This teaching would destroy most of the large fortunes, and even the greater part of the small fortunes of our day. To put it in practice would amount to revolution. But if the teaching is founded in truth, no matter how we may fight against it, it must eventually be put in practice. This is a denial of the absolute right to most property as being in man; and such a denial I hold myself ready to maintain, either by the principles of political economy or of revelation. Does this sound revolutionary?

Revolutionary as this appears, with this thought in another form all Christians are familiar. The book to which we look for our light has always declared: "The earth is the Lord's, and the fullness thereof; the world, and they that dwell therein" (Ps. xxiv. 1); "For all the earth is mine" (Ex. xix. 5); "Whatsoever is under the whole heaven is mine" (Job xli. 11); "For the world is mine, and the fullness thereof" (Ps. l. 12). This truth is quoted in the New Testament, in 1 Corinthians x. 26: "For the earth is the Lord's, and the fullness thereof."

The very basis, then, of Biblical economics is the truth: *God is the absolute owner of the world, and of any particular piece of property in it.* Now it is not remarkable, if revelation be true, that absolute ownership, which belongs to God, cannot be proved to inhere in man. Any given thing cannot belong absolutely to God and to man also. That the voice of pure reasoning, working from largely an atheistic standpoint, and the voice of that book which Christendom regards as the voice of God should unite in the statement that property does not belong to individual man is certainly remarkable. The Bible explains why it does not belong to man: because it does belong to God. The Bible goes farther than these principles of political economy can be pressed, and claims that man himself belongs to God; hence there is in the Bible no difference between the wealth man makes himself and the rest of property. Man belonging to God, what he makes belongs to him, just on the same basis with land and all values.

Now if the title to property rest in God, it can only pass to another by his consent; and any one receiving such title must take it with the limitations put upon it by God, the original owner. These limitations we learn from the Bible, his revealed will. There is no point where it is more clearly revealed than in Luke xvi. 1-12: "And he said also unto his disciples, There was a certain rich man, which had a steward; and the same was accused unto him that he had wasted his goods. And he called him, and said unto him, How is it that I hear this of thee? give an account of thy stewardship; for thou mayest be no longer steward. Then the steward said within himself, What shall I do? for my lord taketh away from me the stewardship: I cannot dig; to beg I am ashamed. I am resolved what to do, that, when I am put out of the stewardship, they may receive me into their houses. So he called every one of his Lord's debtors unto him, and said unto the first, How much owest thou unto my lord? And he said, A hundred measures of oil. And he said unto him, Take thy bill, and sit down quickly, and write fifty. Then said he to another, And how much owest thou? And he said, A hundred measures of wheat. And he said unto him, Take thy bill, and write fourscore. And the lord commended the unjust steward, because he had done wisely: for the children of this world are in their generation wiser than the children of light. And I say unto you, Make to yourselves friends of the mammon of unrighteousness; that, when ye fail, they may receive you into everlasting habitations. He that is faithful in that which is least is faithful also in much: and he that is unjust in the least is unjust also in much. If therefore ye have not been faithful in the unrighteous mammon, who will commit to your trust the true riches? And if ye have not been faithful in that which is another man's, who shall give you that which is your own?"

In this startling parable earthly wealth is but the shadow of true riches; and, such as it is, it is not ours, but another man's—that is, God's; and our possession of the true riches is dependent upon our faithfulness in that which is given us here in trust. Our wealth, then, is not ours to splurge with, to waste in useless extravagance, to use simply as an instrument in the acquisition of more, or to accumulate for our children.

It is a solemn trust, which we hold for the common good. Humanity has an interest in all the possessions of wealth, and it is the dim consciousness that the wealthy classes are not doing the fair thing which is at the bottom of all the trouble of our day.

A man's title to his property is good as against another man. No other man can rightly claim an interest in it, nor can any other determine for him what he must do with it. God has intrusted it to that man, has given him the right over it as against all other men; but has clearly revealed that it is intrusted to him for the good of the human family, and not simply for his own pleasure. It is for him to determine how best to execute his trust; but he dare not ignore it, unless he is willing to rebel against God and wrong man. The very moment that he determines to disregard these claims, and make his wealth subservient to his own ease and comfort, he is in danger of the sentence: "Thou fool, this night thy soul shall be required of thee." By recognizing these facts, we may so use "unrighteous mammon" as by it to make friends for us of God, angels, and good men. And these, when earthly wealth shall have passed away, shall "receive us into everlasting habitations."

This doctrine of stewardship appears also as distinctly set forth in the parable of the talents. Peter clearly teaches it in the following: "As every man hath received the gift, even so minister the same one to another, as good stewards of the manifold grace of God." (1 Pet. iv. 10.)

The teaching of these passages, supported by the whole tenor of the Scriptures, is:

1. Absolute ownership rests in God alone to all property.

2. Man is simply God's steward, set each over a certain part of this vast estate, a tenant at his will.

3. The steward is not to manage this property for his own pleasure, but for God's glory and the good of the race of men.

4. God in the judgment will hold each man to a strict account for the faithful performance of this stewardship.

That this stewardship is to be administered for the race of men is proved by 1 Peter iv. 10, and by Christ's own declaration: "Inasmuch as ye have done it unto one of these my brethren, ye have done it unto me;" "Inasmuch as ye did it not to one of the least of these, ye did it not to me."

Man, then, is identified with God; and the proper treatment of man is recognized as the right use of our stewardship. Here we find another striking agreement between the position of socialists and the deliverances of God's word. The socialist declares the solidarity of the human race, and that all things belong to it, and not to individuals. The Bible implies such a solidarity—in fact, the great doctrines of the fall of man and his redemption rest upon this basis—and while it puts all right to property in God himself, and declares that God intrusts it to individuals, yet he requires the individual to administer it for the *good of the race.*

The right of the individual to property which has come into his hands justly is good as against all individuals. God has given it to him, and no other individual has any right to interfere with this ownership. But he has no title as against God nor has he any as against the race. The whole idea of "eminent domain" rests on the truth that the individual's title to property must give way to the need of the race. But this cannot be set up as showing a distinction between landed property and other forms of wealth; for the laws of all kinds that relate to nuisances, hygienic regulations, and quarantine rest upon the same basis. So all forms of tax recognize the race, as represented by government, as having an interest in all forms of property. These old and fixed principles of government, when traced to their ultimate ground, recognize the fact that the individual's right to property is null as against the race.

CHAPTER V.

THE METHOD OF THE TRANSFER OF PROPERTY TO THE INDIVIDUAL MAN, AND THE CHARACTER OF TITLE HE RECEIVES.

WE have seen that the position of the Bible is that the absolute title to property rests in God. We have seen, also, that God does not pass this absolute title to man, but puts man in possession of property as steward during his life. Man is not owner, but manager. We shall now discuss the manner in which this modified title to property passes into the hands of any man. In God's words to Adam, and afterward to Noah, he gave this world to man as a race. But the race cannot act as a unit; it, in the present state of things, cannot exercise the powers of proprietor. Hence God puts property in the hands of individuals as trustees for the race, holding them to strict account for their faithfulness to the trust. All who are familiar with the Bible know that God thus gave land to man.

We find him giving a part of the earth to Abraham and his seed. We find him afterward dividing this national inheritance out to the families and individuals that compose the nation. He recognizes the title to land as inhering in the individual, though that individual is a female.

God also in his word recognizes the right to personal property. He bestowed great riches upon Abraham and Job and others, consisting for the most

part of flocks of cattle and sheep; and he recognized
their proprietorship. He established laws for the
punishment of any who invaded the rights of a proprietor. He forbids man even to covet—strongly to
desire—any thing which is his neighbor's. Two of
the commandments of the decalogue are based upon
the recognition of the right of exclusive possession
of property by man: "Thou shalt not steal;" "thou
shalt not covet."

The example of the Jerusalem Church is generally
appealed to by all religious communists as showing
that we ought not to own any thing as individuals.
Yet it is in the very midst of the history of this noble example of unselfishness, which was demanded by
the circumstances, that I find the most distinct recognition that this community of goods was not compulsory; and especially of the right of the individual
both to landed and personal property. Let us examine part of this history: "But a certain man named
Ananias, with Sapphira his wife, sold a possession,
and kept back part of the price, his wife also being
privy to it, and brought a certain part, and laid it at
the apostles' feet. But Peter said, Ananias, why hath
Satan filled thy heart to lie to the Holy Ghost, and to
keep back part of the price of the land? While it remained, was it not thine own? and after it was sold,
was it not in thine own power? why hast thou conceived this thing in thine heart? thou hast not lied
unto men, but unto God."

"While it [the land] remained, was it not thine
own?" Here is the strongest possible recognition of
the right to property in land, right in the midst of
the account of the community of property adopted

by this Church, and in the New Testament, God's last revealed will to man. "After it was sold, was it not in thine own power?" Here is a recognition, equally strong, of the purchase money, personal property, in the hands of Ananias as his own, which he might have retained.

The whole Bible recognizes proprietorship on the part of an individual. We wish now to investigate the question, How does he become proprietor of any given property?

A man has reached maturity. His obligations to his father have been canceled. He faces life for himself. He has as yet no property, but he has strong muscles and a sound mind. What does nature say to such a one? "Work or starve." What does political economy say? She indorses the statement of nature. What does the Bible say? "If any man would not work, neither should he eat." In this statement the three are agreed. There is no room for dispute. Our man must work, or he violates the law of his being and the revealed will of his Maker.

God's word comes to him positively and emphatically, saying: "We command and exhort by our Lord Jesus Christ, that with quietness they work, and eat their own bread;" bread which has become one's own because he has earned it by hard work. This settles the question of his joining a noisy, beer-drinking society, and agitating the subject of getting his living by forcing some one else to divide his possessions with him. He must work.

The very moment he accepts this law, and begins honest labor, God's Word says of him, "The laborer is worthy of his hire;" and it denounces the man who does not pay him his wages and the man who pays insufficient wages—even the one who does not pay promptly. The property which he makes by his labor, or the wages he earns, the Bible recognizes as his own.

If day by day he saves a part of his daily wages, until it amounts to a large property, it is still his. He has earned it by the sweat of his brow. The Scriptures defend his title against every comer; but they recognize even this title as a limited one; the absolute title is still in God. That never passes from him. This earning by honest labor, however, gives the best title to the individual to manage for God and humanity this much of the sum of things.

This work that earns wages is not, from a scriptural point of view, simply manual labor. The points where the statement is made in the New Testament, "The laborer is worthy of his hire" (Matt. x. 10, Luke x. 7, 1 Tim. v. 18), are where the right of a minister of Christ to a support is laid down. Here spiritual work, the farthest remove from manual labor, is made the basis for material wages; and this is put into a broad generalization precisely because it was designed to state a truth applicable to all earnest workers, including all brain workers.

Honest work, then, is the first and chief way that God places property in the hands of an individual; but we may recognize all other legal ways of acquisition—by gift, inheritance, bequest, interest, the monopoly of discovery, etc.—as in accord with the divine will; for we have the statement of his word: "For there is no power but of God: the powers that be are ordained of God." This statement was made during the reign of Nero, and shows that government is of God, even when government is at its worst. The man who administers it may be wicked; the laws themselves may not be just; but for that time and that people they are the best that can be done; and obedience to law, even at its worst, is a thousand times better than lawlessness. The enactments of man, acting with proper authority, become the enactments of God.

Hence that property which has come to a man in our day as the result of the action of our laws, as at present constituted, may be accepted as rightly his. This of course does not refer to property accumulated by shirking the law, or evading it, or slipping through its interstices. To such there is only the right of a thief to goods in his possession. Nor does this mean that present laws are right, and ought not to be changed by proper authority; but only that while they are law they should be respected as such; and as the disadvantage of them presses upon all, so any advantage they really bring to any one may be rightly accepted. The law of compensation will thus work to alleviate the inequalities of the system.

We then conclude that any property which has been acquired honestly and legally may be regarded as having been transferred to a man by the divine owner of it, with such limited title as he bestows and subject to such conditions as he affixes to it. If a man accepts the authority of the Bible as the revealed will of God, he is driven irresistibly to this doctrine about property. It is all God's, and he commits portions of it to individuals in these several ways, simply in trust for the good of the race.

Does a man deny the very existence of God, and hence the authority of the Bible? If his position be true, then the socialist is right; man then has no right to any thing which he has not personally earned by his own labor. The derivation of title from God, or from personal labor, are the only tenable positions. The latter position, as we have seen, annuls the title to nine-tenths of the property now held by individuals. If a man takes the only other tenable hypothesis, and claims property under God, then he must be true to his hypothesis not only as a theory perfecting his title as against contestants, but he must put that theory in practice by holding his property in accordance with the character of the title he claims to have obtained. We will restate the character of that title. God puts property in the hands of a man as his agent and trustee, to be used to forward his cause, which is identical with the cause of humanity, and to be controlled by principles which he has laid down for that agent's guidance.

We have seen how property is put in the hands of an individual, and the character of title he gets. It remains for us to try to find the principles which are laid down in God's revealed will for the control of this property. To this we will devote Part II.

PART II.

BIBLICAL ECONOMICS PROPER.

CHAPTER I.

MAN MUST RECOGNIZE HIS STEWARDSHIP.

IF a man is a trustee holding his property from God as principal in trust for humanity, then the very first thing necessary in the management is the recognition of this trusteeship. Though we have already spoken considerable upon this subject in treating of the nature of man's title, yet, both on account of its importance and its relation to the system, it becomes necessary to put it at the head of the principles which God has revealed as required in the management of the earthly estate committed to us.

PRINCIPLE I.—*Whatever we possess we hold not absolutely, but as stewards of God, and in trust for the human race.*

This principle is diffused throughout the gospel rather than packed into quotable formula. The feeling of the poor that they are cheated out of their rights, that they are laboring under burdens and difficulties that their stronger fellows ought to in some way lighten is founded in truth, however much of error may be mixed up in the utterance that gives vent to it. Nor while certain classes, the great majority of the very rich, use their vast possessions as absolutely their own, not only to enjoy and to splurge on, but as an instrument of power to force the public to add to their accumulations, can we expect this discontent to assuage? It will grow with that which feeds it. Wealth must recognize its obligations; or, violating the very conditions upon which it is bestowed, it must expect, sooner or later, to pay the penalty of violated law.

Fortunately, the rich are not all careless of their trust.* The noble gifts to education, to eleemosynary institutions, and to Christian enterprises show that many of them are using their wealth in the right way. The splendid response of Christendom to every case of remarkable affliction by flood or fire or pestilence is as glorious an exhibition of noble action in the present as it is an exhibition of a state of feeling from which we may hope for better things in the future. Our charitable institutions supported by the State, and our whole system of public education, both primary and collegiate, show the wide-spread acceptance of this principle.

An editorial in the *Century* for December, 1885, in "Topics of the Times," under the head, "Mercantilism Transfigured," shows the same thing, and that, too, in the highest intellectual ranks. What is here said of trade is equally true of all methods of money-getting. I give the article entire:

"In that most significant speech made two years ago by President White, of Cornell, to his classmates at Yale, and entitled, 'The Message of the Nineteenth Century to the Twentieth,' the influence on our national life of what the orator aptly describes as 'mercantilism' is most cogently set forth. This 'combination of the industrial spirit with the trade spirit' has been, as he shows, the dominant element in our American civilization. Under its sway there has been a marvelous development of the physical resources of the country, but along with this a too evident decline of the higher forces. The genuine political spirit, the devotion to the public service which leads the citizen to give time and thought to the affairs of the city or State, has been gradually dying out. Men are so consumed with business cares that they find little time or strength for public service. In education and in the cultivation of pure science progress has been made, no doubt; but how little compared with the enormous increase of the national wealth! In literature and art the movement, as he views it, is retrograde, and a good portion of our foremost pulpits are supplied by importations from the Old World. Mercantilism is drawing into its vortex the intellectual strength of the nation. The energies of its most promising young men are enlisted in the pursuit of wealth. Such is the complaint of his own generation made by a man who is by nature an optimist, but who is a careful student of history and a close observer of the manners of his times. 'I believe,' he declares, 'that we shall find that, so far from relatively diminishing, it [mercantilism] is relatively increasing; that, so far from begetting better elements of civilization, it is now beginning to stifle them; that it is now beginning to show itself a despotic element, crushing other elements of civilization which are to add any thing to the earth's history; that, in fact (and I say it in all soberness), mercantilism in great cities and small towns, in society and in the individual, is becoming a disease, certainly feverish, possibly cancerous.' To those who are not too busy with money-making to think much about it, this judgment of existing social conditions will appear to be sane and moderate.

"But these words of faithful warning and reproof are not words of despair. The orator expects that these ruinous tendencies will be checked; that other forces will be evoked to counteract mercantilism and to prevent the 'weakening, decline, and sterility,' toward which it is hurrying the nation. His own prediction of the quarter from which deliverance will come we shall not here repeat, because we desire to make record of a most hopeful answer to the question which he raises, contained in another speech no less significant—an address of Mr. Franklin Mac Veagh, of Chicago, at a dinner given by the Commercial Club of Boston to its guests from the three chief cities of the West.

"The manner of this speech, as well as the matter of it, commend it to all lovers of good literature. After-dinner oratory is not often so graceful. Its delicate wit, its bright allusions, and its deftly turned sentences exhibit a mind of fine grain and careful culture. It would be hard to find a professional talker, East or West, who could put his thoughts into a better form. Evidently here is one man who, though he proclaims himself a trader, has contrived to extract some sweetness from the barren pastures of mercantilism.

"But the art of the performance does not hide its purpose. The business man's responsibility to society is the serious theme on which he finally lights, and the view which he takes of the matter leaves nothing to be desired by patriot or philanthropist. The estimate of the trader's function here laid down, if it were accepted by all business men, or even by the better part of them, would speedily correct those evil tendencies of which Mr. White has warned us.

The Chicago trader protests, indeed, against the undue disparagement of the mercantile vocation. 'Trade,' he says, 'is a much abused benefactor. It would not do to take seriously the foppish views of trade held by the idle end of society. To them nothing is dignified but idleness. This mediæval survival of prejudice is chiefly cherished by the useless part of the nobility and their admirers in America, by that part of the *noblesse* whom the English wit must have had in mind when he made his classification of the "men of ability and the men of nobility."'

"The dignity of any calling depends, first, upon its aims; secondly, on the qualities developed in its pursuit. 'Let us frankly admit,' this orator goes on to say, 'that the aims of trade have not been all that they might have been. But what, on the other hand, shall we not claim for those high qualities of mind and character, for the untiring enterprise, the wise judgment, and the undaunted courage that from the very beginning of history have made commerce the bearer of civilization from every center to every circumference; that made her the origin of cosmopolitan life, the solvent of the antagonisms of custom, the necessary foundation for every enlargement of the life of nations? And shall we not now claim that the ideals, the aims of trade are widening and deepening? Is it not true that men more and more are associating with the dream of wealth a sense of public responsibility and an aspiration for public usefulness? And is it not true that the good works of the nation largely depend upon the intelligent sympathy and co-operation of business men?'"

If these last questions can be confidently answered

in the affirmative, the future of this nation is secured. And it is certainly a good sign that from one of our chief centers of business activity should come so full and strong a statement of a doctrine that offers a solution of the gravest questions now before us. We quote in full the next two paragraphs of this noteworthy speech:

"It is a great temptation, Mr. Chairman, now that I have gotten so far on the way, to go ahead and claim that we men of affairs are altogether perfect. But a reluctant honesty obliges me to confess that before we shall be quite all that we might be to the world, wealth must be sought still more generally for its good uses. Of course men must be left free to accumulate property for their own purposes. A form of society which should prevent the free accumulation and possession of property would simply stagnate progress, and is impossible. But, on the other hand, it is not difficult to believe that the avenues to exceptional wealth can only be held by the few, as at present, through the intervention of important concessions to that spirit of democracy which is entering upon a new stage of its mastery of the world; for democracy, after all, is not more a governmental revolution than it is a social revolution. The greatest concession, it seems to me, that will be demanded of wealth by democracy—a concession that will answer the demands of progress as well—will be frank acknowledgment of the moral trusteeship, of a moral obligation to freely use surplus wealth for the general good.

"Happy the necessity, beneficent the tyranny that will thus rule trade and wealth to their own glorious enfranchisement. When such an acknowledgment is generally made, wealth and trade shall be lifted up to the level of the highest and the best. Once inspire trade with such an aim, free wealth from its spiritual bondage through this great ideal, give to all the pursuits of business such a right royal sanction that they shall take rank and dignity with all the work that is done by humanity in its best estate, with poetry, with every form of literature, with every form of art, with statesmanship, with apostleship; and Crœsus, hugging his millions to his bosom as his own, in the narrow sense of ownership, rejecting the idea of trusteeship, will be overwhelmed in the rush of the current of modern ideas. Crœsus accepting the idea of trusteeship will be the new force in civilization for which the world is waiting.

"We ask whether there be not condensed into these two paragraphs from the speech of the Chicago 'trader' more solid statesmanship, more true insight into existing social conditions, a wiser solution of the greatest question of our time, than was contained in all the stump speeches of the last presidential campaign. The prediction here uttered respecting the challenge which a militant democracy will soon be flinging at the feet of a too confident plutocracy is one that may well be heeded. And the answer that Mr. Mac Veagh proposes to make is the right answer. Such a recognition of moral trusteeship as he urges will pluck the sting from socialism, and save to the world the fruits of enterprise. Mercantilism, transfigured through these higher aims, will cease to be the peril of the State, and become its protection and defense."

We have here at once the opinion of a great educator on the evils growing out of the present methods of getting and holding riches, and we have the opinion of an eminent man in literature agreeing with a practical business man, each looking at things from their own stand-point; and the opinion so eloquently set forth is simply a noble call for the recognition of the principle here presented—the trusteeship of man. And they rightly regard the recognition of this first principle laid down by Christ as a long step in the direction of solving all the difficulties and problems that now perplex our civilization. In fact, the editor of the *Century* thinks the living up to this one principle would bring perfect peace to a world sadly troubled. Is it not remarkable that the opinions of the very ripest scholarship and of experienced trade, looking for a solution of our present industrial difficulties, should coincide with the principle announced by the Galilean peasant nineteen centuries ago?

In the exercise of this trust it is not demanded that a man forget himself entirely. As the accumulator of wealth he has a kind of first right to its benefits. "Thou shalt not muzzle the ox that treadeth out the corn" is quoted as a general principle by Paul in an argument proving that the minister of the gospel has a right to share in the good he brings to the world. It is still more applicable to the wealth-getter. He has a right to spend upon himself so much of his wealth as is really necessary for his own well-being—physically, mentally, socially, morally, and spiritually.

Then a man's family are more directly the ones for whom he is responsible. "If any provide not for his own, and specially for those of his own house, he hath denied the faith, and is worse than an infidel." It is after these immediate claims are met that the claim of humanity at large comes to be a valid one. But the pressing character of the demand for help must enter into the determination of a given case. For instance, the necessity of a starving stranger would take precedence of some comparatively unimportant want of a man's own child.

In the very nature of the case the needs of the cause of Christ must have first claim upon his steward, unless offset by great and pressing counter claims. Dr. J. D. Barbee well says in a sermon on Luke sixteenth chapter that a man is but the cashier in the Almighty's bank; and when God draws a check, he dares not dishonor it. After listening to this sermon one of the most consecrated laymen, a rich man who is God's child, remarked to the writer that the central idea of trusteeship was all right; "but," he asked, "who is to decide as to the genuineness of that check?" Here is where many make a mistake. They imagine that it is the man who presents a claim upon another, whether in the name of the Church or of himself, who is to decide the character of the check. It is the man who is on the inside of the window, and not the one who is on the outside, on whom the responsibility rests. "To his own master he standeth or falleth." Let selfishness beware, however, how it refuses to cash the check which its own conscience accepts, and how it "lies unto God."

The full and joyous recognition of the fact by a man that he is but God's steward is, in large measure, the fulfillment of the first and great commandment: "Thou shalt love the Lord thy God with all thy heart, and with all thy soul, and with all thy mind."

CHAPTER II.

Love Thy Neighbor as Thyself.

HAVING now the correct conception of our relation to our property, we are ready to further investigate the laws laid down in the Bible, directing in the control of wealth. The next great principle, and the chief one in the management of fiscal affairs, so far as they relate to our fellow-men, is the Second Commandment, which is like unto the first:

PRINCIPLE II.—"*Thou shalt love thy neighbor as thyself.*"

Of this great principle Paul makes the following exhaustive statement: "Love worketh no evil to his neighbor: therefore love is the fulfilling of the law." Law here is used not, of course, in the sense of ceremonial or Mosaic law, nor in that of the imperfect enactments of human governments; but it is used in the sense of the ideal, the perfect requirements of God as to man's reciprocal duties, which have not yet been embodied in human statutes, and which are epitomized in the one word "love." Here is the key to all our difficulties; here is the divine solution of the problems. There can be no more marked contrast between the rich and the poor, nor no relation between the employee and the employer, which wrenches the right adjustment between them more violently awry than that between Philemon and Onesimus, the master and the slave of Roman days. But all the friction and the hardness is taken out of even this relation by this gracious law of love, which requires Philemon to receive his slave as "a brother beloved both in the flesh and in the Lord."

The troubles with us do not grow out of our relations to one another, nor mostly (though partly) out of our imperfect laws, but out of the spirit in which we meet one another.

The old and selfish maxims of political economy, which have done their own peculiar service to civilization, have also brought to fruitage in our day a bountiful crop of evil. Man is naturally selfish. That the law of love may be operative it is necessary that a great change be wrought in him. Political economy proposes to nurture man's innate selfishness, and to guide it wisely to its selfish aims. The Bible proposes to eliminate selfishness, and to supply its place with benevolence. Yet this benevolence is not to ignore or oppress self. We are to "love our neighbors as ourselves," not more than self; we are to love them as ourselves, not as we do a wife or a child or a personal friend. It puts their interests and our own in perfect equipoise. This is God's plan for removing all friction.

How far we are from accepting this wonderful plan is seen by a mere glance about us. Christian era as this is, it is pre-eminently the day of selfishness. I know all about our eleemosynary institutions, and our increased gifts and work for the Church. These show that the Spirit of Christ is not dead: they are hopeful signs. But I am speaking now of our money matters—pure business, as it is termed. Here selfishness reigns almost supreme. The principles of Christ are beautifying our homes, purifying our society, and ennobling our lives as a race; but we still allow the selfish maxims of an infidel political economy to rule in matters of money-making. So true is this that in our day we find the enigma of a man grinding his employees by small wages to save money to give to benevolent enterprises. The one is business; the other is religion. The two are kept separate.

All this the Bible demands shall be changed. Our dealings with one another must be on this basis of love. Surely we have outgrown the barbaric state where every one looks upon his fellow as his natural enemy, and is watching him to prevent being overreached; yet it is precisely this that the philosopher and the clown recommend—the one in truth-seeming *formulæ*, and the other in such homely proverbs as, "Every tub must stand on its own bottom." This is a state of active warfare between those who should be brothers. This is destructive, and not constructive. Mutual help growing out of mutual love is the constructive principle in human society; and just so far as these have been allowed to rule has civilization been built, and no farther. "Love one another" is the only solvent that will break up the tendency in our nation to crystallize into hostile classes—the farmers arrayed against merchants, tradesmen against lawyers, and wage-workers against all the rest. But we will return to this subject under the third principle.

I know of no place where the nature of selfishness and the efficiency of the divine remedy for it have been so forcibly presented as by Mr. Harris in his wonderful book, "Mammon;" and I take pleasure in giving his eloquent words to the reader, as exactly voicing what I am trying to set forth:

There is, be it observed, a wide difference between selfishness and legitimate self-love. The latter is a principle necessary to all sentient existence. In man it is the principle which impels him to preserve his own life and promote his own happiness. Love to God and our neighbor does not annihilate, but rather cherishes a regard to our own highest good. True piety gives this regard the right direction, and guides it to seek supreme happiness in God. It is the act or habit of a man who so loves himself that he gives himself to God. Selfishness is fallen self-love. It is self-love in excess, blind to the existence and excellence of God, and seeking its happiness in inferior objects, by aiming to subdue them to its own purposes.

Accordingly selfishness, as we have already intimated, is the prevailing, not to say universal, form of human depravity; every sin is but a modification of it. What is avarice but selfishness grasping and hoarding? What is prodigality but selfishness decorating and indulging itself—a man sacrificing to himself as his own god? What is sloth but that god asleep, and refusing to attend to the loud calls of duty? What is idolatry but that god-enshrined man worshiping the reflection of his own image? Sensuality, and indeed all the sins of the flesh, are only selfishness setting itself above law and gratifying itself at the expense of all restraint. And all the sins of the spirit are only the same principle, impatient of contradiction, and refusing to acknowledge superiority or to bend to any will but its own. What is egotism but selfishness speaking? or crime, but selfishness, without its mask, in earnest and acting? or offensive war, but selfishness confederated, armed, and bent on aggrandizing itself by violence and blood? An offensive army is the selfishness of a nation embodied and moving to the attainment of its object over the wrecks of human happiness and life. "From whence come wars and fightings among you? Come they not hence even of your lusts?" And what are all these irregular and passionate desires but that inordinate self-love which acknowledges no law and will be confined by no rules, that selfishness "which is the heart of depravity?" and what but this has set the world at variance, and filled it with strife? The first presumed sin of the angels that kept not their first estate, as well as the first sin of man—what was it but selfishness insane; an irrational and mad attempt to pass the limits proper to the creature, to invade the throne, and to seize the right of the Deity? And were we to analyze the very last sin of which we ourselves are conscious, we should discover that selfishness, in one or the other of its thousand forms, was its parent. Thus, if love was the prevailing principle of the unfallen creation, it is equally certain that selfishness is the reigning law of the world, ravaged and disorganized by sin.

It must be obvious, then, that the great want of fallen man is a divine remedy for selfishness, the epidemic disease of our nature. The expedient which should profess to remedy our condition, and yet leave this want unprovided for, whatever its other recommendations might be, would be leaving the seat and core of our disease untouched. And it would be easy to show that in this radical defect consists the impotence of every system of false religion, and of every heterodox modification of the true religion, to restore our disordered nature to happiness and God. And equally easy is it to show that the gospel, evangelically interpreted, not only takes cognizance of this peculiar feature of our malady, but actually treats it as the very root of our depravity, and addresses itself directly to the task of its destruction; that, as a first effect of sin was to produce selfishness, so the first effect of the gospel remedy is to destroy that evil, and to replace it with benevolence.

It is the glory of the gospel that it was calculated and arranged on the principle of restoring to the world the lost spirit of benevolence. To realize this enterprise of boundless mercy, Jehovah resolved on first presenting to mankind an unparalleled exhibition of grace; an exhibition which, if it failed to rekindle extinguished love in the heart of man, should at least have the effect of kindling anew the raptures of angels and seraphs around his throne. The ocean of divine love was stirred to its utmost depths. The entire Godhead was (if with profound reverence it may be said) put into activity. The three glorious subsistencies in the divine essence moved toward our earth. Every attribute and distinction of the divine Nature was displayed: the Father, the Son, and Holy Spirit embarked their infinite treasures in the cause of human happiness.

"God so loved the world, that he gave his only begotten Son, that whosoever believeth on him should not perish, but have everlasting life." He could not give us more; and the vast propensions of his grace could not be satisfied by bestowing less. He would not leave it possible to be said that he could give us more; he resolved to pour out the whole treasury of heaven, to give us his all at once. "Herein is love;" love defying all computation; the very mention of which should surcharge our hearts with gratitude, give us an idea of infinity, and replace our selfishness with a sentiment of generous and diffusive benevolence.

Jesus Christ came into the world as the embodied love of God. He came and stood before the world with the hoarded love of eternity in his heart, offering to make us the heirs of all its wealth. He so unveiled and presented the character of God that every human being should feel that God can be "just and the justifier of him that believeth in Jesus." "He pleased not himself." He did nothing for himself; whatever he did was for the advantage of man. Selfishness stood abashed in his presence. "He went about doing good." He assumed our nature expressly, that he might be able to suffer in our stead; for the distinct and deliberate object of pouring out his blood, and of making his soul an offering for sin. He planted a cross, and presented to the world a prodigy of mercy of which this is the only solution: that he "so loved us." "While we were yet sinners Christ died for us." He took our place in the universe, espoused our interest, opened his bosom, and welcomed to his heart the stroke which we had deserved.

And in all he did, he thought of the world. He loved man as man; he came to be the life and light of the world; he came and stood as the center of attraction to a race of beings scattered and dissipated by the repulsive power of selfishness. He proposed by the power of the cross to "draw all men unto him." His heart had room for the whole race; and, opening his arms, he invited all to come unto him. The whole of his course was a history of pure and disinterested benevolence; one continued act of condescension; a vast and unbroken descent from the heights of heaven to the form of a servant, the life of an outcast, the death of a malefactor. His character is a study of goodness, a study for the universe; it is the conception of a being of infinite amiableness, seeking to engage and enamor the heart of a selfish world.

The world having lost the original idea of goodness and sunk into a state of universal selfishness, his character was calculated and formed on the principle of a laborious endeavor to recall the departed spirit of benevolence, and baptize it afresh in the element of love.

The office of the Holy Spirit is appointed and concurs to the same end. The world could not be surprised out of its selfishness and charmed into benevolence by the mere spectacle even of divine love. That love can be understood only by sympathy; but for this, sin had disqualified us. According to the economy of grace, therefore, the exhibition of that love in God is to be made the means of producing love in us; the glorious spectacle of love as beheld in God is to be turned into a living principle in us. For this end, the holy, unconfined, and infinite Spirit came down. His emblem is the wind; he came like a rushing, mighty wind; came with a fullness and a power, as if he sought to fill every heart, to replenish the Church, to be the soul of the world, to encircle the earth with an atmosphere of grace as real and as universal as the elemental air which encompasses and circulates around the globe itself, that whoever inhaled it might have eternal life.

In the prosecution of his office he was to take of the things of Christ, and show them unto men. Heaven stooping to earth; God becoming man, dying upon the cross; infinite benevolence pouring out all its treasures for human happiness—these were the things which he was to reveal, the softening and subduing elements with which he was to approach and enter the human heart. In his hands these truths were to become spirit and life. From the moment they were felt, men were to be conscious of a change in their relation both to God and to each other. A view of the great love wherewith he had loved them was to fill their minds with the grand and overpowering sentiment of benevolence which should melt their obduracy, cause them to glow with gratitude, and bind them fast to himself in the strongest bands of love. That love, with all the communicativeness of fire, was to extend to their fellow-men. Every weapon of revenge was to fall from their hands; every epithet of anger was to die upon their lips; and where, before, they saw nothing but foes they were henceforth to behold most noble objects of affection, immortal beings, whom it would be happiness to love and Godlike to bless. The love of Christ would constrain them; glowing and circulating in their spiritual system, like the life-blood in their hearts, it would impel them to be active for his glory. Having communed with the heart of infinite Love, they were to go forth and mingle with their race, filled with a benevolence like that which brought their Lord from heaven. Placing themselves at his disposal, they were to find that they were no longer detached from the species, but restored and related to all around; the sworn and appointed agents of happiness to the world. . . . .

Thus the Christian Church, like the leaven hid in the meal, was to pervade and assimilate the entire mass of humanity. At first it would resemble an *imperium in imperio*, a dominion of love flourishing amidst arid wastes of selfishness; but, extending on all sides its peaceful conquests, it would be seen transforming and encompassing the world. Combining and consecrating all the elements of moral power, it would move only to conquer, and conquer only to increase the means of conquest. It would behold its foes converted into friends; then, assigning to each an appropriate station of duty, would bid him forthwith go and try upon others the power of that principle which had subdued his own opposition: the omnipotent power of love. Thus thawing, and turning into its own substance the icy selfishness of humanity, the great principle of benevolence would flow through the world with all the majesty of a river, widening and deepening at every point of its progress by the accession of a thousand streams, till it covered the earth as the waters cover the sea. They who, under the reign of selfishness, had sought to contract the circle of happiness around them till they had reduced it to their own little center, under the benign and expansive influence of the gospel, would not only seek to enlarge that circle to embrace the world, but to multiply and diffuse themselves in happiness to its utmost circumference. Feeling that good is indivisible, that to be enjoyed in perfection by one, it must be shared and possessed by all, they would labor till all the race were blended in a family compact and were partaking together the rich blessings of salvation; till, by their instrumentality, the hand of Christ had carried a golden chain of love around the world, binding the whole together, and all to the throne of God.

It is clear, then, that the entire economy of salvation is constructed on the principle of restoring to the world the lost spirit of love. This is its boast and glory. Its advent was an era in the universe. It was bringing to a trial the relative strength of love and hatred—the darling principle of heaven, and the great principle of all revolt and sin. It was confronting selfishness in its own native region with a system of benevolence prepared, as its avowed antagonist, by the hand of God himself; so that, unless we would impugn the skill and power of its Author, we must suppose that it was studiously adapted for the lofty encounter. With this conviction, therefore, we should have been justified in saying, had we been placed in a situation to say it: "Nothing but the treachery of its professed friends can defeat it. If they attempt a compromise with the spirit of selfishness, there is every thing to be feared; but let the heavenly system be worked fairly, and there is every thing to be expected: its triumph is certain." ("Harris's Mammon," passages from Sections II., III., and IV.)

Here, then, is the state of feeling in which God intends man to meet man. Without this love no arrangement of the relations of men, however perfect, can prevent discord and trouble. With this love there is no relation, however defective, but what can be made to produce mutual happiness.

CHAPTER III.

MUTUAL CONSIDERATION, MUTUAL HELPFULNESS, AND DOING ALL WORK AS UNTO GOD.

THE law of love is of universal force and dominates all other principles that I shall present. It is the general law, and each of the others is the special manifestation of it. This love of one another must manifest itself in mutual consideration, which comes as our third principle.

PRINCIPLE III.—"*Whatsoever ye would that men should do to you, do you even so to them.*"

This requires that in every act involving a fellow-being I am to try to look at it from his stand-point as well as my own. I am to treat another just as I would be treated by him. This breaks down a narrow, selfish view of things and leads to a broad, unselfish view, which is always not only the more correct, but the more advantageous. It is the narrow selfishness of a Charles the First which loses him his head, and of a George the Third that loses him an America. It is the calm and equitable consideration of others' interests and rights which gives a William of Orange or a Washington an exalted place in history.

One of the greatest difficulties under which civilization now labors is this looking at every thing from this stand-point of self, which shows itself especially in the present tendency to view every law or social problem from the stand-point of a class or a section. The employers co-operate together to accomplish what they suppose will benefit them as employers, however it may affect the interests of others. The employees band themselves together to resist what they consider oppressive and to work for their own good. The farmers look at every thing as it affects agriculture. So with each of the classes composing the body politic and of that peculiar organism of our day, the incorporated body. All are endeavoring to gain a personal or a corporate, a class or a sectional advantage; and use all their power, including the ballot and pressure upon legislative bodies, to that end. Hence we find mighty cleavages in the body politic, showing a tendency to break up into classes—a disintegration which if it continues can only result in death. It is already a disease. For this disease with which we are now suffering and which threatens such fearful results and ravages in the future the principle of which we are now treating is the only remedy as it is in any circumstances the only wise course. So intimately are we related, so inter-dependent are we, there can be no healthy condition for society which is not an advantage to all its elements; and there can be no class oppressed and ground down and suffering but what society at large will be afflicted accordingly.

The rich employer then must consider the condition and the interest of his poor employee. The manufacturer who gives the weak sewing-woman a mere pittance for making a shirt, a pittance altogether insufficient for her needs, does a cruel wrong which cannot be atoned for by donating the profits on that shirt to charity. No employer has a right to any profit until those who work for him have been justly and fairly treated. To simply look at the labor supply and get work at the cheapest possible price is to look at things from only the stand-point of his own interests and to ignore the other side. For a man to give grossly insufficient wages to those dependent upon him for a support ought to be as infamous as robbery or theft; it is as wrong. Nor is it any more excuse to say that you cannot afford to do better and have a fair interest on the capital than it would be for a merchant to declare that he could not make a sufficient per cent. upon his goods without cheating in weights and measures. Necessity is no excuse for crime, especially for a rich man to whiningly plead it as an excuse for grinding the poor while his own luxuries are yet untouched.

But the employee must be just to the employer also. He must in his demands take into consideration all that affects both parties, the state of the market, a fair return upon investments, the necessity for repairs, etc. And for a set of employees, fairly paid and justly treated, to grasp after more and to take advantage of circumstances to force it from the employer is also a palpable sin. "Look not every man upon his own things, but every man also upon the things of others." I do not know but that this last passage is a more exact statement of the great truth which I am now trying to enforce than the one I have chosen as a formula for Principle III. In either case all that I have here said is fully justified by the words of infinite wisdom.

This law is not only applicable to persons and classes, but also to nations. All laws intended to act to the disadvantage of other nations and the advantage of our own are wrong in principle; and as all of

God's laws are self-executing, the nation that throws a Chinese wall about itself by unjust tariffs must, sooner or later, suffer from this disregard of principle.

The great principle of love will not stop at merely being just. It must sweep on beyond these narrow boundaries into the wide regions of mercy, "whose quality is not strained." Hence we have

PRINCIPLE IV.—*"Bear ye one another's burdens."*

We must not only be mutually considerate: we must, if necessary, be mutually helpful. The needs of our fellow-man must waken in us a desire to help, and this desire must go forth in active effort. Every man is a brother, and we must do by him a brother's part. Christ has set this principle before us in an illustration so aglow with light and radiant with mercy that, familiar as it is, I will give it here entire, rather than hunt up some inferior illustration myself:

"And, behold, a certain lawyer stood up, and tempted him, saying, Master, what shall I do to inherit eternal life? He said unto him, What is written in the law? how readest thou? And he answering said, Thou shalt love the Lord thy God with all thy heart, and with all thy soul, and with all thy strength, and with all thy mind, and thy neighbor as thyself. And he said unto him, Thou hast answered right: this do, and thou shalt live. But he, willing to justify himself, said unto Jesus, And who is my neighbor? And Jesus answering said, A certain man went down from Jerusalem to Jericho, and fell among thieves, which stripped him of his raiment, and wounded him, and departed, leaving him half dead. And by chance there came down a certain priest that way; and when he saw him, he passed by on the other side. And likewise a Levite, when he was at the place, came and looked on him, and passed by on the other side. But a certain Samaritan, as he journeyed, came where he was; and when he saw him, he had compassion on him, and went to him, and bound up his wounds, pouring in oil and wine, and set him on his own beast, and brought him to an inn, and took care of him. And on the morrow when he departed, he took out two pence, and gave them to the host, and said unto him, Take care of him: and whatsoever thou spendest more, when I come again, I will repay thee. Which now of these three, thinkest thou, was neighbor unto him that fell among the thieves? And he said, He that showed mercy on him. Then said Jesus unto him, Go, and do thou likewise." (Luke x. 25-37.)

Wherever the cry of distress is heard we are to hasten to its relief. No prejudice, nor bigotry, nor class-feeling is to make us shut our ears to humanity's appeal or fail to respond to humanity's needs.

But we are not to carry this to the point of injuring the object of our charity. We are not allowed to needlessly indulge self in idleness or to so indulge one of our family. Still less is it right for us to support any in idleness who have no other claim on us than that of common humanity.

The next economic principle which we find in the Bible is as follows:

PRINCIPLE V.—"*All service or work should be done as unto the Lord, and not unto man.*"

This is the rule laid down for even slaves, but it runs through all manner of service. There is nothing more severely condemned than "eye service." According to this principle, a laborer, for instance, in a shoe-factory is to regard his work as a God-appointed task, and he is to do it as unto Christ; and he may rightly look not only for wages from his employer, but also, if he has rightly performed his work, for a reward hereafter from his Maker. Thus we see the employer's interests are protected, as are also those of the future consumer. In this way every task would have conscience put into it.

This view dignifies and ennobles all human labor. Our man in the shoe-factory is doing a work for humanity and for God. The right performance of that work glorifies his Maker and benefits his fellow-man. If the work is improperly done, it may bring great suffering in its wake. Suppose that he has something to do with putting the soles upon shoes. Hundreds of them pass through his hands daily. Through his carelessness a certain per cent. of this number are cut in handling and are thus rendered leaky. But he conceals the mischief done, and these defective shoes are sold with the rest. Now follow a pair of these shoes to the market in some distant town. There a poor sewing-woman has been hoarding her savings to buy her winter's shoes. She has enough now to buy a cheap, machine-made pair, stout and warm. With what joy she makes the purchase and lays the old pair aside and puts upon her wearied feet that bright new pair! She dares to brave the snow and slush now in the prosecution of her work. But, alas! she has one of those injured shoes, and she comes home with cold, wet feet instead of the warm, dry ones she expected. This gives her a severe cold, which settles upon her lungs and develops into consumption.

Through that long winter she works and coughs and drags her wearied body around in a dreary effort to support her little ones. Then in the spring she takes her bed, and others have to support her and hers. And some bright day in May they lay her wasted, lifeless frame "under the daisies," and some homeless waifs are left to take their chances in the world. All this because a man without a conscience made the soles of her shoes. George Herbert well says:

> Who sweeps a room as for thy laws
> Makes that and the action fine.

CHAPTER IV.

Discontent and Love of Money Condemned.

THE word of God comes to us with these great principles prescribed for our guidance. And if these positive principles are regarded, if they become ingrafted in our natures, changing them into a likeness to the divine nature, then the very motive to evil is eliminated and we need no further law or exhortation. Then the "peaceful fruits of righteousness" shall so manifest themselves that the verdict of all observers shall be, "Against such there is no law," human or divine. But the Bible, the product of Him who "knew what was in man," does not stop with the revelation of these positive principles which, if observed, would meet the case, but it goes on to prohibit all that will lead to the opposite result. It comes down to restless, striving, foolish man, and it raises its voice in warning against those principles and practices which have introduced discord, confusion, and every hateful crime among men. Seeing the great, struggling mass of humanity ready to do almost any thing to change their state, the Bible comes and says authoritatively:

PRINCIPLE VI.—*"Having food and raiment, let us be therewith content."*

If man would listen to this voice, how the storms that rage about us would quiet down! "Food and raiment" represent almost all of material goods that can confer any real good upon the race. If the poor man in good health, with a wife and children making glad his humble cottage, and with enough of wages to supply daily wants, knew it, he has no cause to envy any man any thing. The discontent of which Horace sung, however, is still characteristic of our race. It is still approximately true: "No man lives content with that lot in which fortune has placed him." It is this discontent, growing out of the exaggerated ideas about the happiness of other men, which is a peculiar characteristic of our age. The restless mass move backward and forward, seeking a paradise upon earth and finding it not. Each class imagines that the others have the advantage of them, and they grow dissatisfied over imaginary wrongs.

Now our principle recognizes that when man's legitimate wants are met then discontent is not only useless, but positively wrong. Up to the time that a man's honest work brings him enough to feed and clothe himself and his loved ones, there is no demand that he be satisfied; but the very moment that this is done, then the Word forbids him uniting his clamor to the universal cry for more. It does not forbid him making legitimate efforts to rise into a better condition. Ever onward and upward it would have him forge ahead. But this is a very different thing from that restless discontent which is here condemned. The one is the mighty impulse, God-implanted, which ever moves mankind forward into wider plains; the other is the perversion of this impulse into a wild rage that would tear down all the marks of progress heretofore made by the race.

PRINCIPLE VII.—*"If riches increase, set not your heart upon them."*

An inseparable part of that spirit of dissatisfaction of which we have just treated is the feverish desire for riches, which is a marked characteristic of our day. Every one wants to be rich, and few are willing to wait for the ordinary methods to lead to this yearned for goal. Nothing but evil can come of this inordinate thirst for riches. Never was there a time when the world needed to listen more attentively to the warning words of Paul: " But they that will be rich fall into temptation and a snare, and into many foolish and hurtful lusts, which drown men in destruction and perdition. For the love of money is the root of all evil; which while some coveted after, they have erred from the faith, and pierced themselves through with many sorrows. But thou, O man of God, flee these things; and follow after righteousness, godliness, faith, love, patience, meekness. Fight the good fight of faith, lay hold on eternal life." We have already quoted the words of President Elliott, showing that he regarded this as the great evil standing in the way of our progress as a nation in all the higher walks of life.

Every man of thought, who has not himself been bitten by this universal craze for money, sees in it the mightiest foe to our well-being. From this " love of money " as a root there is springing up a terrible crop of evil, threatening destruction to Church and State and our whole social fabric. This inordinate desire for wealth leads to all manner of crime against the rights of our fellows. God's Word comes and forbids the very desire out of which these things grow; and this takes in those who have nothing as well as those who have great wealth. But as a matter of fact the "increase of riches" increases the temptation to "set the heart upon them," and adds to all the temptations to get them improperly and to hold them contrary to the law of God. Hence James gives this exhortation and warning, especially to the rich: "Go to now, ye rich men, weep and howl for your miseries that shall come upon you. Your riches are corrupted, and your garments are moth-eaten. Your gold and silver is cankered; and the rust of them shall be a witness against you, and shall eat your flesh as it were fire." The Saviour raises his voice in gentle warning, saying solemnly, "Take heed, and beware of covetousness." He tells us emphatically that "it is easier for a camel to go through the eye of a needle, than for a rich man to enter into the kingdom of God," and he means exactly what he says. There is no exegesis that can make these words mean less than the impossible. But Christ says that with God all things are possible, even this. What does this whole remarkable passage mean? In my opinion it sets forth the true doctrine of wealth and our relation to it. Christ intends to teach that so long as a man holds his wealth as his own, to do as he pleases with, so long it is impossible to enter the kingdom of heaven. He must make a complete surrender of himself and all he has before he can enter the "strait gate." He cannot give himself to God, and keep his riches to himself. He must unstrip himself of all his belongings, and turn them over to God; and then he can come in, and then only. Does this mean that he is to give away all his possessions before he can obtain eternal life? No; but it does mean that he recognizes his true relation to his wealth, that he accepts the divine statement that the wealth is God's, and that he is simply God's agent to manage it for the good of mankind. The very moment that he honestly accepts this fact he is as poor a man as any one. If a poor but honest man has a vast estate put in his hands as trustee, to manage for a family of minors, is he then rated as a rich man? Precisely this is man's true relation to his wealth. When he adjusts himself to this truth, he is then in a savable state; but he is in reality no more a rich man, as the world counts riches. But so long as he refuses to accept this truth, so long it is simply an impossibility for him to become a Christian. Riches are a great responsibility and a great trust, and a knowledge of their true character would take out of the human heart the feverish and hurtful anxiety to obtain them.

Is it wrong, then, for man to try to obtain wealth? If he tries only in the proper manner, and then uses what he obtains as a trust to be managed for the good of man, then it becomes a noble act. There is no point where God needs workers in his vineyard more than right here, and there have been no class of workers so slow to put themselves in the hands of Christ. The *entrepreneur* (the master of finance) sees so clearly all the material advantages, is so powerfully impressed with the earthly, that it has always been difficult to keep him from setting his heart upon riches, and so refusing to put himself in the hands of God or to surrender the results of his enterprise to the divine uses. Among the very twelve Christ laid his hands upon one of these clear-headed men of affairs. He needed him in his great work. But he proved unfaithful to his high trust. When Judas recognized the lofty talents of the Saviour, and saw his mighty power, he concluded that he was the coming Messiah, and he followed him as such. When the people tried to make Christ king, and he not only refused, but in that fearful arraignment of them recorded in John vi. set forth the spiritual character of his mission, there was one clear brain and sharp eye that saw farther than John or Peter. Judas, I think, saw there how easy it would have been for Christ to organize the nation at that crisis, and place himself on the throne. He understood, also, that he taught that such an earthly kingdom was foreign to his intention. He saw, further, that the course which Christ deliberately chose would lead to a conflict with the Jewish hierarchy and with the Roman power. He seems to have resolved then and there that if Christ was determined to thus involve himself in sure destruction he would not follow him in the fool-hardy course. Why do I think that he determined at this time what his course should be? Because at the close of this record in John we have this: "Jesus answered them, Have I not chosen you twelve, and one of you is a devil? He spake of Judas Iscariot the son of Simon." This is the first that we hear of any thing wrong among the apostles, because it was here that the germ of his final betrayal was planted.

Why do I believe that Judas was an able man, a man of affairs? In the first place, he was actually the financier of that company. He was their treasurer; he managed their affairs. Nor was it any small thing to provide for all the wants of a company of at least thirteen. Again, if I am right about the genesis of his crime, then the very reasoning which led to the crime showed his remarkable penetration. He alone so far back in the ministry of Christ caught the fact of the purely spiritual character of his kingdom. Then the betrayal itself was a shrewd piece of work. If by putting him in the hands of his enemies he forced him to use his mighty power to destroy his foes, and to assume openly the power and prerogatives which Judas saw he possessed, then Judas simply gave him the opportunity to assert himself. If Christ continued his meek policy, and for unaccountable reasons went down before his enemies, then Judas had made friends with the other side, and so would escape the ruin which he now considered it impossible to avert unless Christ called to his aid his divine power, which he could do as well as a prisoner as under any other circumstances. Then his thrifty nature discloses itself in making all he could out of the transaction, on which he had doubtless determined independent of the thirty pieces of silver.

I have dwelt thus far upon Judas because the subject is in itself interesting, and because I believe it shows that God tried at first to get an *entrepreneur* among his workers, and failed. Then you remember the young man who came to him, and Jesus loved him? But when Christ, who knew him, placed before him the choice of salvation or his wealth, the young man went away sad. I believe that here again Christ tried to get one of these clear-headed men to do his work, and failed; because he who has exceptional power to manage the affairs of this world always finds it hard to surrender it for that world which lies so far away and seems so shadowy to their practical brains.

Thus down through the ages the Spirit has been

reaching out for a great manager of the fiscal affairs of the kingdom; and a glance at the money devoted to pleasure, to business enterprises, and to all manner of selfish work will show any one that this class of men have either held themselves aloof from the Lord's work, or that they have devoted but a *modicum* of their talents or their means to his service. Humanity, civilization, and the Church stand more in need of men who will make a right use of their talents in money-making than of any other character of workers for the race; and this talent has been more withheld from the use of humanity and of God, and more perverted to the purposes of Satan, than any other gift which Providence has bestowed upon ungrateful man; and the possessor of this talent has been too much led to believe that the very exercise of his peculiar power was somehow at variance with God's law. Hence in the very determination to follow his natural impulses he settles the question of following what he believes to be right. His very determination to make money involves the idea in his mind that he was going to do wrong; hence he puts himself at the start out of harmony with right living, and of course henceforth he ignores the claims of right. Now I would come to every man specially endowed with this power to manage financial affairs, and I would say to him: "God wants you to exercise your gift; and so long as you make money rightly, and so long as you use it when made according to your best judgment and conscience for the benefit of the race, you are doing one of the greatest works ever given to humanity to perform."

CHAPTER V.

DELAY OF PAYMENTS TO LABORERS, STEALING, UNFORGIVENESS, AND SABBATH-BREAKING FORBIDDEN.

SUCH emphasis has been put in the Bible upon the subject of proper payment of those whose services we secure that I shall put the following as my next principle:

PRINCIPLE VIII.—"*The wages of him that is hired shall not abide with thee.*"

In the passage from which this principle is quoted it is forbidden to delay the hireling's wages even until the morning. God's whole word forbids keeping back any part of what another has earned by his work, or even slow payment to needy laborers. In Deuteronomy xxiv. we have: "Thou shalt not oppress a hired servant that is poor and needy. . . . At his day thou shalt give him his hire, neither shall the sun go down upon it; for he is poor, and setteth his heart upon it: lest he cry against thee unto the Lord, and it be sin unto thee." This sin of wronging laborers out of their work brought forth from the stern old Hebrew prophets some of the most fearful denunciations that ever fell from their lips. Take this passage from Jeremiah xxii.: "Woe unto him that buildeth his house by unrighteousness, and his chambers by wrong; that useth his neighbor's service without wages, and giveth him not for his work; that saith, I will build me a wide house and large chambers, and cutteth him out windows; and it is ceiled with cedar, and painted with vermilion. Shalt thou reign, because thou closest thyself in cedar? did not thy father eat and drink, and do judgment and justice, and then it was well with him? He judged the cause of the poor and needy; then it was well with him: was not this to know me? saith the Lord. But thine eyes and thy heart are not but for thy covetousness, and for to shed innocent blood, and for oppression, and for violence, to do it. Therefore thus saith the Lord concerning Jehoiakim the son of Josiah king of Judah; They shall not lament for him, saying, Ah my brother! or, Ah sister! they shall not lament for him, saying, Ah lord! or, Ah his glory! He shall be buried with the burial of an ass, drawn and cast forth beyond the gates of Jerusalem." These words were re-echoed by James, when in a burst of indignation against the unworthy rich he declares: "Behold, the hire of the laborers who have reaped down your fields, which is of you kept back by fraud, crieth: and the cries of them which have reaped are entered into the ears of the Lord of Sabaoth."

Such are the terms used in God's word against those who wrong those who have worked for them. They express the highest kind of reprobation. It is more probably insufficient pay rather than no pay at all that is so fearfully denounced. As we have seen, the very slightest wrong against the workman, such as delay in payment, is forbidden, and has the strong terms "robbery" and "fraud" applied to it. God's eyes are on the poor, and his ears are ever open to their cry. He who oppresses or defrauds them shall surely awaken his wrath.

PRINCIPLE IX.—*" Thou shalt not steal."*

This command is too well understood to call for any elaborate treatment here. What belongs to one man God has told all other men to let alone. So exceedingly jealous is he of the rights of property that in another of the Ten Commandments he forbids us to covet any thing that is our neighbor's. These two commands cover all possible methods of getting the property of other people without an equivalent.

Specially, as has been pointed out recently by a writer, is all sorts of gambling and lotteries forbidden by this eighth commandment. The *London Methodist Times* speaks as follows:

> It will be within the recollection of many of our readers that Mr. Bradfield demonstrated in an admirable paper, which we had the privilege of publishing, that gambling stands in precisely the same relation to stealing that dueling stands to murder. In both cases the victim is a willing victim, and takes his chance of being the victor. But the enlightened opinion of these days does not excuse a duelist murderer because the man he has murdered consented to the arrangement and did his best to be the murderer. In the same way, a gambler cannot be excused because the confederate whom he fleeces is a consenting party. In that case also the consent of the victim does not alter the moral character of the act. However unworthy the victim may be of sympathy or pity, the gambler is none the less to blame in the sight of God and of all who rise above the imperfect and conventional morality of our semi-barbarism. We believe that no effectual restraint will be placed upon the practice of gambling until every gambler, be he prince or peasant, is branded as a thief.

Then among short-sighted and hasty-tempered men, one of the most important principles is this:

PRINCIPLE X.—"*Forgive, if ye have ought against any.*"

So important is this that Christ declares: "But if

ye do not forgive, neither will your Father which is in heaven forgive your trespasses." It is made a *sine qua non* to salvation. Nor is this overstressing the necessity for this virtue. It is human to want to get even. That my opponent has stopped his injuries is not enough for my injured pride, not even when he is sorry for his misdoing. He has made me suffer, and he too must suffer. This is man's feeling. But God meets this wrathful spirit with an emphatic "don't." And he so emphasizes this command as to assure man that his own salvation is directly involved in his forgiving his enemy. How this pours oil upon troubled waters!

PRINCIPLE XI.—"*The seventh day is the Sabbath of the Lord thy God: in it thou shalt not do any work.*"

Six days are granted unto man to attend to the affairs that belong to economics, but the seventh is absolutely forbidden for this purpose. It is the time for attending to the interest of the soul exclusively, while the tired body and mind rests for its tasks in the coming week. The claims of this day, however, are not put above human need, but wherever there is real human necessity there we are authorized to treat the Sabbath as any other day. But this must be a work of genuine necessity, not a money-making scheme. Man has no real right to property earned by breaking the Sabbath-day. These express companies that make such a fuss over the stealages of some of their employees are but reaping where they have sown. They have taught men to set aside one of the laws of God; it is no wonder that they teach them to set aside another. And the thieving clerk has as much right to the property he gets as the company has to that which has been earned on the Sabbath.

God is cheated out of the worship due him, and man is cheated out of his proper rest, whenever the Sabbath is used as a common day of work. All good citizens should unite with the wronged workmen who are forced to break the Sabbath, and see to it that every American has a day of rest.

CHAPTER VI.

SOME ABSOLUTE SOCIOLOGICAL LAWS.

WE have discussed in previous chapters the principles which the Bible requires to be observed in our dealings with men and our management of our private affairs. In this chapter I propose to treat of certain fixed principles which the Bible reveals as existing in the realm of human activity just as gravity, density, and others exist in the realm of physics. All that man can do in these cases is to learn the law and conform himself to it. His action in the premises can have no effect upon the law itself. The reckless man who ignores gravity and leaps from a precipice is simply crushed into a shapeless mass at its feet, but the great law is unchanged and the general order of nature undisturbed. So a man may neglect these great laws; but if so, he does it at his own peril. He cannot alter, he can only conform.

These principles are as follows:

I.—*"To him that hath shall be given."*

Like it if we do or do not, there it stands, as true, as solid, and as awful as Gibraltar. The advantage of having is not, as many suppose, the result of legislation, but is in the very nature of things. Neither can it be altered by legislation. Yet this is precisely what the short-sighted agitator of our day is generally trying to do—change the unalterable law of God: "To him that hath shall be given."

Let me illustrate. We will suppose that a man owns

160 acres of land and puts a fence of four planks around the whole tract. His poorer neighbor has a tract of just sixteen acres. That is just one tenth as much as the other. He too must protect his property with a fence, we will suppose of the same character. The richer man will have to provide a fence containing 21,120 feet of lumber, and this at $10 a thousand for his lumber will amount to $211.20, or $1.32 per acre. Now our poorer man must use 6,679 feet of fencing at a cost of $66.80, or $4.17 per acre. Our richer man has ten times as much land as the other, but it takes only 3.17 times as much to fence it; and we see by the above figures that the poorer man has to bear a larger tax by $2.85 per acre than his neighbor.

This is in the nature of things, and cannot be altered. Nor is this an unusual incident. Take the price of wood by the cord and by the fifty cents' worth and work it out, and you will find something very similar. Does this look strange? Let us look then at the next one of these great principles:

II.—"*From him that hath not shall be taken.*"

Things act to the advantage of the man that has. But no less certainly they act against the man who has not. A man has to buy on credit. Calculate the per cent. he pays over and above the cash customer. Nor is this an injustice, as he is sometimes disposed to believe; but in the very nature of things. The merchant who sold only at a fair price to his cash customers and yet gave his credit ones the same bargains would soon be in the hands of the sheriff. I care not where you turn, you will find the man who has not laboring under peculiar disadvantages. These disadvantages are sometimes unaccountable, but they are invariably there. We will suppose I am looking out for a wood-chopper. A man comes along without an ax and wants the job; but as I have none, I am compelled not to give it to him. He and his babes, perchance, go supperless to bed that night. Another comes along with an ax and secures the job, earning money to meet his needs. The difference between them was the possession of $1.50, but it meant much. Had the two men come together, and had I possessed an ax, I would certainly have given the job to the man who came with his tool for work with him, for the tool of the one bespoke the workman and the absence of it would suggest the tramp.

These principles seem harsh at first, nor are we able to fully understand their wisdom; but God has revealed in connection with them his method of equalizing things. "For unto whomsoever much is given, of him much shall be required." Certain burdens are to be borne for the race. God adjusts these burdens to the strength of the parties. Man can do nothing but follow the divine example and adjust the burdens of society and government upon this principle. The rich, having in the nature of things the advantage, should be made to bear the great burden of supporting society; while the poor man should be left to take care of himself and family and keep them from becoming a burden upon society either as paupers or as criminals. Yet our tariff laws do the exact opposite of this. They burden the poor man out of all proportion to his rich neighbor. In fact, this policy not only neglects this divine plan, but it disregards the next one of these great principles.

III.—*"Whosoever will save his life shall lose it."*

Does man rebel against the divine arrangement by which all the powers of his being and all the products of his labors are devoted to God and the benefit of the human race? and does he endeavor to wrest them to his own use and enjoyment? The effort is absolutely in vain. He may take his life out of the service of the Almighty, but he may rest assured that it, or just so much of it as he endeavors to devote to his own exclusive use and enjoyment, is absolutely lost. By the unvarying law of God, acting beyond the reach of man's strength or will, selfishness is doomed to thwart its own purposes and destroy itself. Who that has watched the play of forces in the field of sociology does not see the working of this mysterious law? A narrow, selfish policy is always unwise and always leads to undesirable results. The seeming exceptions are only exceptions in appearance. Nemesis is on the track of the would-be rebel against the divine economy, and sooner or later it will overtake him; and the longer any judgment of this court is in being executed the more fearful the day of reckoning when it does come.

This is as true of nations as it is of individuals. Here too those who seek only their own advantage, and disregard and set aside all the claims and rights of others, are sure to lose the very thing they make such elaborate efforts to save. Now, as I have said, the tariff laws of the United States utterly disregard this great law. They are the very embodiment of national selfishness. They throw themselves directly in the path of the irresistible forces of the universe, and sooner or later they must be crushed by the power they defy.

Already our merchant marine has been driven from the seas; already the marts of merchandise at our very doors are nearly monopolized by foreign traders; already our agricultural classes are being crushed by the reaction of these laws against their products and the increase of the price of all that they buy. It will be well for us if we take warning in time, and, by changing our policy, avoid the results of violated law, for there is a place for repentance in all these things. I believe that there is not a single wrong suffered by society, not a perplexing problem pressing for solution, not a dangerous cloud darkening our political sky, but what it is intensified by these tariff laws.

A glance at history verifies the law laid down by Christ. Did the Jews reject the unattractive spiritual kingdom he offered them, and proceed to try to set up a kingdom upon earth which should magnify the Jews and humiliate their foes? They simply committed national suicide. Their scattered people and desolated cities were God's answer to the effort to "save their life."

Did the proud Roman ignore every thing but his own pleasure? Their great families literally rotted in moral corruption, their proud aristocracy was swept from the earth, and the reins of the world fell from their nerveless hands. They proved recreant to their trust, and the trust is taken from them.

The kings of the earth used their high authority and place to indulge in all kinds of vice, luxury, violence, and tyranny; and not as a great trust to be used to advance human happiness and welfare; and their headless bodies and crownless heads stand as monuments to the unwisdom of their course; while the very name of one of their greatest families, Bourbon, has become a by-word and a sneer, representing a folly too great to learn any thing from misfortune. God has written it all along the course of human history: selfishness is the surest road to self-destruction. He has declared it in his Word. Yet men are too dull to see or believe.

So much of every man's life as is kept from the use of the race and devoted to his own service is embezzled, and God therefore declares: "Whosoever will save his life shall lose it."

IV.—*"It is more blessed to give than to receive."*

Not only has God so emphatically denounced selfishness and so clearly revealed its folly. He has also declared the blessings of unselfish benevolence. Unselfishness acts to the real best interest of self. Nor does this mean that when we reach the world of spirits we shall find that unselfishness is there so rewarded as to make it the best and wisest course. It is so here and now. Instead of that portion of our life that we devote to others, to God, and to humanity being taken from self, the Saviour says: "Whosoever shall lose his life for my sake shall find it." The last fragment of life that is devoted to these high purposes shall react in a mysterious way for the emolument and advancement of self. Do Livingston and Stanley, in devotion to the wants of humanity, leave civilization behind, with all its tempting prizes and its joys, and bury themselves in African jungles? Some day they wake up to find themselves the world's heroes, and they are astonished to find civilization waiting to crown them with such wreaths as are never bestowed upon one who has not given his life, or risked it, for her. So universally does unselfishness work to the advantage of an individual that the noblest works of self-abandonment are often disparaged by the accusation that they were the work of far-sighted selfishness which saw the advantage it was to reap. Have you ever noticed the orator, conscious of himself and trying to show what excellent things he could do? What a ridiculous figure he cuts! But let that orator forget himself, and try to move and benefit men, and be so absorbed in his theme as to be oblivious of himself, and how almost godlike he becomes! So it is with every human act. It only acts for the good of self when it is the outcome of a nobler thing than selfishness.

Of all objects in nature the flowering shrub seems to most devote itself to the benefit of the world without doing any thing for itself. Its beautiful flowers spread themselves abroad to delight other eyes, and it pours out its perfume on the sweet-scented air to refresh each passer-by. But these very things which are thus generously given to others are the qualities that attract the pollen-laden insect that fructifies its blooms, and so secures vigorous seeds to perpetuate itself. In revelation, history, and nature God utters this truth.

V. *"A man's life consisteth not in the abundance of the things which he possesseth."*

Man is greater than his possessions, and he is not the mere creature of his environment. Environment can never make a man; it cannot unmake a true man. Many of the reforms now being pressed proceed upon the false principle that if you improve man's condition you improve him necessarily. This reverses the facts. Improve man, and he will improve his own condition. The projects that propose to revolutionize the world, morally, by simply revolutionizing the relations and conditions of mankind are simply chimerical.

Man may disbelieve in all these absolute laws here presented, and disregard their execution. They move right on; and if man gets in their way, so much the more they show their power. Legislation and custom make no difference. They stop not to consult with man, individually or collectively. They execute themselves. As free and as unvarying as the mighty forces that move the stars, they go on their way; and man can do nothing but adjust himself to them, or be crushed in their path.

Here we have set forth in these principles that should control our conduct, and in these laws that do control in sociology, the economic doctrines of the Bible. Who can devise a better political economy? Have we not here the very basis for a science that the wise have been hunting for? A political economy written from this stand-point will give us a science of economics as it ought to be; and if such a work recognizes the actual existence of the conflicting principles of selfishness, and the modification of the power of love resulting therefrom, then we would have a work true to the facts as at present found in the field of sociology.

The world has calmly assumed that these great principles of the Bible are suitable for some ideal Utopian state, but utterly unfit for our work-a-day world; and the Church itself has, in practice at least, accepted this position as true. On the contrary, these principles are eminently practicable; they will work, and work to the highest ends of the individual and of the body politic.

Is it contended that they are only practicable in a world converted to Christ? I answer that the monetary affairs are in the hands of Christian nations now, and mostly under the domination of professedly Christian people. Are these things waved aside contemptuously, as only fit for Utopia? I answer that in the providence of God we have arrived at a point where we must make this earth—at least our great republic—an Utopia, or it will become an Erebus.

PART III.

WHAT REVOLUTION SHALL IT BE?

CHAPTER I.
Revolution Imminent.

THE evidences that the present order of things is more and more unsatisfactory to the masses are constantly accumulating. Murmurs deep and loud are heard on every hand. If those who imagine that things must go on forever as they now are will study history and mark the signs of the times, they will see an alarming number of things presaging revolution.

Look at the marvelous development of the vastly rich in our nation. Read Dr. Strong, or better, Mr. Thomas G. Shearman in the *Forum*, and weigh their words well. The latter says: "Making the largest allowance for exaggerated reports, there can be no doubt that these seventy names [which he had just given] represent an aggregate wealth of $2,700,000,000, or an average of over $37,500,000 each. . . . The facts already stated conclusively demonstrate that the wealthiest class in the United States is vastly richer than the wealthiest class in Great Britain. The average annual income of the richest hundred Englishmen is about $450,000; but the average annual income of the richest hundred Americans cannot be less than $1,200,000, and probably exceeds $1,500,000."

How rapidly both extremes of society, the very rich and the very poor, are increasing among us! Mark, too, how these rich are combining in trusts and soulless corporations; and how they control our legislation and dominate our politics. The political parties, indeed, court the poor man publicly, but all know that they are controlled by the rich. This plutocracy is getting to be something terrible. The luxury and the extravagance and selfishness of our rich, their utter disregard of any obligation upon their part toward society, make a situation naturally dangerous still more so. Now listen to Carlyle in his "French Revolution:"

In fact, what can be more natural, one may say inevitable, as a Post-Sans culottic transitory state, than even this? Confused wreck of a republic of the poverties, which ended in reign of terror, is arranging itself into such composure as it can. Evangel of Jean-Jacques, and most other evangels, becoming incredible, what is there for it but return to the old evangel of Mammon? Contrat-social is true or untrue, brotherhood is brotherhood or death; but money always will buy money's worth. In the wreck of the human dubitations, this remains indubitable, that pleasure is pleasant. Aristocracy or feudal parchment has passed away with a mighty rushing; and now, by a natural course, we arrive at aristocracy of the money-bag. It is the course through which all European Societies are at this hour traveling. Apparently a still baser sort of aristocracy? An infinitely baser; basest yet known.

In which, however, there is this advantage, that, like anarchy itself, it cannot continue. Hast thou considered how thought is stronger than artillery parks, and (were it fifty years after death and martyrdom, or were it two thousand years) writes and unwrites acts of Parliament, removes mountains, models the world like soft clay? Also how the beginning of all thought, worth the name, is love; and the wise head never yet was without first the generous heart? The heavens cease not their bounty; they send us generous hearts into every generation. And now what generous heart can pretend to itself, or be hoodwinked into believing, that loyalty to the money-bag is a noble loyalty? Mammon, cries the generous heart out of all ages and countries, is the basest of known gods, even of known devils. In him what glory is there that ye should worship him? No glory discernable; not even terror: at best, detestability, ill matched with despisability! Generous hearts discerning, on this hand, wide-spread wretchedness, dark without and within, moistening its ounce and half of bread with tears; and, on that hand, mere balls in flesh-colored drawers, and inane or foul glitter of such sort, cannot but ejaculate, cannot but announce: Too much, O divine Mammon; somewhat too much! The voice of these, once announcing itself, carries flat and pereat in it, for all things here below. ("The Guillotine," Book VII., chapter vii.)

Now turn to the other extreme—the poor, the idle, the worthless, and the wretched. Listen to their murmurs and their curses deep and loud. Read again in Carlyle:

But fancy what effect this Thyestes repast and trampling on the national cockade must have had in the Salle des Menus in the famishing bakers' queues at Paris! Nay, such Thyestes repasts, it would seem, continue. . . . Yes, here with us is famine, but yonder at Versailles is food, enough and to spare. Patriotism stands in queue, shivering, hunger struck, insulted by patrollotism, while bloody-minded aristocrats, heated with excess of high living, trample on the national cockade. Can the atrocity be true? Nay, look—green uniforms faced with red, black cockades—the color of night! Are we to have military onfall, and death also, by starvation? For, behold, the Corbeil corn-boat which used to come twice a day with its plaster-of-Paris meal, now comes only once. And the town-hall is deaf, and the men are laggard and dastard! At the Cafe de Foy, this Saturday evening, a new thing is seen, not the last of its kind—a woman engaged in public speaking. Her poor man, she says, was put in silence by his district, their presidents and officials would not let him speak. Wherefore she here, with her shrill tongue, will speak, denouncing, while her breath endures, the Corbeil boat, the plaster-of-Paris bread, sacrilegious opera dinners, green uniforms, pirate aristocrats, and those black cockades of theirs!

Truly, it is time for the black cockades at least to vanish. Then pattrollotism itself will not protect. Nay, sharp tempered "M. Tassin," at the Tuileries' parade on Sunday morning, forgets all national military rule, starts from the ranks, wrenches down one black cockade which is swashing ominous there, and tramples it fiercely into the soil of France. Pattrollotism itself is not without suppressed fury. Also the districts begin to stir; the voice of President Danton reverberates in the Cordeliers. People's friend Marat has flown to Versailles and back again— swart bird, not of the halcion kind.

And so patriot meets promenading patriot this Sunday, and sees his own grim care reflected on the face of another. Groups, in spite of pattrollotism, which is not so alert as usual, fluctuate deliberative—groups on the bridges, on the quais, at the patriotic cafees. And ever; as any black cockade may emerge, rises the many voiced growl and bark, A bas (down)? All black cockades are ruthlessly plucked off; one individual picks his up again, kisses it, attempts to refix it, but "hundred canes start into the air," and he desists. Still worse went it with another individual, doomed by extempore plebiscitum to the lantern; saved with difficulty by some active Corps de Garde. Lafayette sees signs of an evervescence, which he doubles his patrols, doubles his diligence, to prevent. So passes Sunday the 4th of October, 1789.

Sullen is the male heart, repressed by pattrollotism; vehement is the female, irrepressible. The public speaking woman at the Palais Royal was not the only speaking one. Men know not what the pantry is when it grows empty, only house mothers know. Old women, wives of men that will only calculate and not act! Pattrollotism is strong, but death by starvation and military onfall is stronger. Pattrollotism represses male patriotism; but female patriotism? Will guards named national thrust their bayonets into the bosoms of women? Such thought, or rather such dim, unshaped raw material of a thought, ferments universally under the female night-cap, and by earliest day-break on slight hint will explode." (F. Rev., ¶¶ 536-540, of Book VII., iii. The Bastile.)

Then look again at the combination of all classes into societies, well-organized and ably officered. Mark the numbers on their rolls, and note their enthusiasm. Read again:

Revolution Imminent. 113

Where the heart is full, it seeks, for a thousand reasons, in a thousand ways, to impart itself. How sweet, indispensable, in such cases, is fellowship; soul mystically strengthening soul. . . . In such a France, gregarious reunions will needs multiply, intensify; French life will step out of doors, and, from domestic, become a public club life. Old clubs, which already germinated, grow and flourish; new everywhere bud forth. It is the sure symptom of social unrest: in such way, most infallibly of all, does social unrest exhibit itself; finds solacement and also nutriment. In every French head there hangs now, whether for terror or for hope, some prophetic picture of a New France: prophecy which brings, nay which almost is, its own fulfillment; and in all ways, consciously and unconsciously, works toward that.

Observe, moreover, how the Aggregative Principle, let it be but deep enough, goes on aggregating, and this even in a geometrical progression; how when the whole world, in such a plastic time, is forming itself into clubs, some one club, the strongest or luckiest, shall by friendly attracting, by victorious compelling, grow ever stronger, till it become immeasurably strong; and all the others, with their strength, be either loving absorbed into it, or hostilely abolished by it. This if the club spirit is universal; if the time is plastic. Plastic enough is the time, universal the club spirit: such an all-absorbing paramount, one club cannot be wanting. (C. F. R., ¶¶ 704–706.)

Is this not descriptive of our day? Are not all these premonitions of a coming storm about us? Are they not indications that we will have a revolution unless there be a reformation? Such is the opinion of the leading thinkers in economic circles. Read the following from Professor Ely: "Economic science has shown us the possibility of better things for the masses, and we cannot rest quietly with things as they are. Our responsibility for conditions which have been mentioned is something we feel in spite of ourselves. We may deny it, we may ask indignantly, 'Am I my brother's keeper?' but down deep in

8

our hearts and consciences we feel this responsibility, and even while denying it we show that we feel it by our acts and by our conversation."

Change, then, being imminent, it becomes both interesting and profitable to try to discover what change will be for the better; for if the better plan is not adopted, the worse will be forced upon us. Let us then carefully examine the various revolutions and reforms which have been proposed, and weigh their relative merits.

CHAPTER II.

Revolution Proposed in Co-operation.

THERE are a large number of thinkers in economic science who believe that all the friction between capital and labor can be done away with by co-operation. This combines the capitalist and laborer in the same person, and makes that person interested in the profits of the money and the work which have been put into any given product.

The proposition is simply this: A large number of poor men are to unite, and by taking stock in a given enterprise are themselves to furnish the capital necessary to put say a large manufactory in operation. These stockholders are supposed to be experts in the proposed work, and they also become the operatives. They elect their managers, bosses, book-keepers, salesmen, and all employees other than the regular operatives. One man, then, furnishes one kind of work, and another a different kind; and of course their pay will differ in proportion to the responsibility and difficulty of the task. However, when it is all really under way, the income will be used to first pay all employees; and then, if a surplus is left, it will be divided as dividends among the stockholders. According to this system the employers engage themselves to do the work. The same parties are employers and employees, and, in the very nature of things, there is no room for any friction. If each of these persons were an intelligent, unselfish, industrious, efficient, and honest man, there would be a good chance of success in this project; but, as man is now constituted, I confess that I see little light in this direction. There seems to me to be almost insuperable difficulties to the scheme, both internal and external. I invite the reader to follow me in a careful consideration of these difficulties.

The first difficulty in these days of vast enterprises, carried on by great accumulations of capital, will be found in the securing of sufficient capital in this way to accomplish any thing. We might say that in manufacturing to-day $1,000,000 is the average capital necessary to make an enterprise sufficiently strong. Now to find one thousand laborers of the same kind, with $1,000 each, will be found a difficult thing in practical life. It would be still more difficult to find a larger number of them with smaller amounts to invest.

Should we succeed in organizing our enterprise, we would yet be by no means through with our trouble. We would encounter still greater difficulty in the actual operation. Here, in fact, I must believe that, unless these thousand men were totally different from the ordinary men gathered promiscuously, almost insuperable difficulty would interpose. Some of these men would be ambitious, and they would have a higher opinion of themselves than any one else; and when others were taken for the more responsible and the better paid positions, they would become envious and cause more or less friction. Others could not be made to see the reason why the places of least manual labor should have the best pay.

Again, we would find some lazy stockholders who

would not do their share of the work; but as they held stock, it would be difficult to get rid of them. The same problem would be presented by the drunken laborer. Though he had impaired his productive capacity below the average, it would be found much more difficult to get rid of him than in the ordinary case. Of course they would have the right to buy out objectionable parties; but each man would be found to have his friends, and they would make a fight for him; and all this would cause division, friction, and disorganization. Some years ago the writer knew of a serious strike in a large railroad shop, because the boss discharged a drunken workman. It seems to me that co-operation must increase rather than diminish the friction incident to discharging workmen.

Should the management prove inefficient, or for any cause unsatisfactory, the trouble growing out of an effort at change would be still greater.

Again, should those who manage the funds of the concern prove dishonest, it would be easy to defraud men unfamiliar with finance and book-keeping. The few managers might readily combine to fleece the many stockholders.

It may be asked if the same difficulty is not incident to all stock companies. Not so much so, from the fact that large enough blocks of stock are in the hands of skilled financiers, who keep a careful lookout for their interests. In this case such men, in the very nature of the case, would be absent.

Nor is it likely, again, that these workmen would pay salaries sufficient to command first-class talent for the management of their affairs. This would put them in poor shape to meet competition in the field.

But this brings us to the consideration of the external difficulties in the way of co-operation. They would have to meet in the field of competition vast capital ready to fight for its life. This capital would resort to all plans to cheapen their product to a point below the power of the co-operative concern to follow. They would cut down the wages of their workmen. The removal of a large number of the better fixed laborers from the open market, while they are still at work in productive manufacture, would put the remainder, who would be unable to get work in the co-operative establishment, more than ever in the power of the capitalist class. Should these laborers strike, they would soon learn that, for all practical purposes, their stockholding brethren had become capitalists; for we can scarcely suppose that they now would unselfishly help to support their striking brothers, when there is no prospect of their needing such help themselves.

The capitalists would also use women and children's labor, wherever practicable. Again, having friends among all other classes of capitalists, they would secure, in spite of law, advantages over the co-operatives in fuel, freight, and other respects.

Again, the capitalists' concerns, being managed from the top by a compact and skilled set of men, to whom the highest officers are responsible, and who are themselves independent of these officers, would naturally be more efficiently managed than concerns whose managers had all the large number of stockholders more or less in their power. The result of all this would be that the capitalists would undersell the competitors in the market; and that means that the co-operatives would sooner or later be driven from the field.

These reasons seem to me conclusive in proof that co-operation would not meet the emergency, so long as man is not vastly greater and better than he now is. It is to be noted that the difficulties we see are almost all traceable to human wickedness.

I have no doubt that co-operation on a small scale, and not assuming proportions of such magnitude as to provoke especial opposition from capital, would be moderately successful; but such a small scale business would accomplish nothing toward solving our problem.

There is a modified form of co-operation which is proposed. In this the capitalist owns and runs his factory, but he voluntarily gives his operatives a part of the profits of the business, in addition to the wages of the men. This would be a wise and politic plan, but such a slight adjustment of things would by no means do away with friction or banish all difficulty. Selfish and exacting employers would still clash with unreasoning employees, while generous and wise men can operate the present plan without serious trouble.

CHAPTER III.

THE REVOLUTION PROPOSED BY HENRY GEORGE IN LAND OWNERSHIP.

AS to Henry George's proof that man can have no absolute title to land, we have seen that this is true of other property as well. Absolute title is in God alone.

As to his proposed land tax, considered as a plan for the simplifying of our tax system and equalizing the burdens of government, there is no special objection. A single tax has much in its favor. As a wise and equitable method of raising money for the support of the State it commends itself to the judgment. A single tax would be a vast improvement on our present system of complex taxation.

But this is not really Mr. George's system. This is intended only as a stepping-stone to something else. He proposes to tax land to the full extent of rent. He proposes that the government shall receive from land all that the landlords in country and city now receive for the whole land property of the country, not including improvements. It is a long jump toward socialism. This is not to say that it is necessarily wrong, but it is to say that it changes the whole principle of government and society. This of course should not be done, unless for grave reasons. It would raise by taxation a sum far beyond the necessities of the government. This sum would be spent for the benefit of the masses, in some way not clearly revealed. It would belong to the whole State, and it would be distributed in some manner so as to do away with poverty, want, and vice. How this is to be done so as to not administer to laziness I have not been able to make out.

Peculiar difficulty will be found in the inauguration of this reform, if it is pressed in the form of confiscation of landed values. The capitalist, the farmer, the owner of his home in town and city, will be found a solid wall in opposition. Now there must be powerful arguments introduced to prove to these parties that the surrender of their property on their part will operate to the public good to an extent that will justify their personal sacrifice, before their patriotism can be made to outweigh their individual interests. It is folly to talk of the homeless taking this right from them without their consent. The land owners and their natural allies are the rulers of this country, and what is done must be done with their consent. I believe that it would not be an impossible task to secure this consent if it could be shown that the proposed reform was based in equity and would work to the advantage of the whole State, including of course the former land owner.

Can this be done? Let us point out some reasons why it cannot. Having shown that the land owner's title to land is derived from God, just as in the case of other property, and that it rests on as secure a basis as any other property, it follows as a matter of course that its owners cannot be made to see that it is equity for them to surrender their possessions to other people—precisely because it is not equity. The conscience of good men shows them nothing wrong in the ownership of land and no difference between that and their other possessions, nor has the excellent reasoning of Henry George aroused this conscience to the realization of any such wrong. Christian men consider that their very endowments of mind and body belong to God, and that they must be used for the good of the race. They put their ownership of land on the same basis; hence it is impossible to arouse their conscience on this subject, unless you can first miseducate the conscience. Now no revolution can stand any chance of success in our country unless it bases itself upon the Christian conscience of our people. This being an impossibility in this case renders it improbable that even the experiment will ever be tried.

The objections, however, to this plan, were it inaugurated, are many. In the first place, one of the noblest and most beneficial sentiments in the human breast is the love of home. This sentiment is closely related to the ownership of that home. This owning of a home on the part of any man has a tendency to make him a conservative member of society. Then it ministers to the disposition to improve and beautify the home of the family. The experience of the race thus far is that the ownership of land in common, even though the improvements be individual property, is an interference with this home sentiment on the one hand, and totally subversive of the tendency to improve the premises on the other. Go to the Indian Territory and see the workings of this principle. Excellent farm lands—with their farm-houses, barns, etc., mere temporary shells—show the timidity of man in putting improvements on property unless the title is invested in himself. Nor is this the result of their being in the hands of Indians, who care for none of these things. Many fine farms are in the hands of cultivated people, in part or wholly white.

Now cross the Red River into Texas, and note the difference in farm and village improvements, and take another object lesson in the same study of human nature to the same purport.

If the surplus revenue of government derived from the immense tax on land is devoted to the support of the indigent classes, the result will be to vastly increase the pauperism of the nation. Mr. George talks as if poverty was to be no more, and that because of the direct distribution of this surplus to the needy classes. ("Progress and Poverty," pp. 395, 396.) The pauper spirit is one of the most hateful and demoralizing things to which man is addicted. It is itself a vice. It destroys manliness and independence, and makes man a dependent without spirit and without any noble quality. As a pastor, familiar with poverty and the efforts to relieve it, I regard the spirit of the pauper as one of the things to be most dreaded and avoided by the individual man, and most earnestly worked against by the State and by all who are interested in the development of the race. And every one who is at all familiar with pauperism knows that it is increased in direct proportion to the efforts made to provide for the wants of men without requiring work as an equivalent. The free distribution of food and necessities on the occasion of great calamities, such as that at Johnstown, has demonstrated that such free gifts, even in these extreme cases, are demoralizing.

The chief difficulty, however, is in the management of this immense estate by the government officials. The existing executive would have to determine the questions of the amounts to be distributed to the beneficiaries, and who shall be those beneficiaries. The different political parties would vie with each other in courting the floating vote by pandering to them. Then the fiscal officers would handle immense sums of money. All this would afford occasion for great corruption and wide-spread demoralization. Not yet has the government arisen into whose hands such power could be safely intrusted. Nor does the present state of political ethics justify the hope that it will speedily rise.

Nor has Mr. George proved that such a confiscation of land would result in the equalization of distribution. Many, perhaps most, of the causes of the present inequality in sharing the benefits of increased wealth would still exist. Perhaps the chief of these is the superior talent for organization possessed by some individuals over their fellows. Sometimes a man organizes a mercantile establishment, as Wanamaker or Stewart; sometimes he gambles successfully in stocks, as Fisk; sometimes he organizes railroad enterprises, as Gould or Huntington; sometimes he shows his superiority by inventions, as Field or Bell or Edison; sometimes by eminence in professional life, as Evarts or Butler. Nor would the remedy reach the most dissatisfied set of laborers we have, such as the railroad hands, etc.

Still less would this remedy have any effect in removing the greatest cause of poverty and suffering that we have -- *i. e.*, vice and crime. In fact, the very difficulties of the present state of things, the small margin of the workmen this side of actual want, makes against vice, as it insures such immediate fearful consequences to follow the vicious course. But if we were to succeed in putting the laboring-man as far from the immediate consequences of sin as the fashionable dude now is, it would increase and not diminish vice. This statement accords with the best economic thinking, and with the economic history so far as that has been recorded.

While such provision for support would postpone the immediate consequences of vice and diminish the deterrent effects of those consequences, yet it is not in the power of man to remove these consequences. They would come to the front in spite of every effort. The consequences of vice would be what they have always been: misery and woe and want. A mightier power than men has decreed that this hateful brood shall follow in the wake of sin, and man has never wasted his time more foolishly than in his efforts to abrogate the laws of the Almighty.

I will not close this chapter without saying that Mr. George has done much good by his writings, and has thrown much light upon many problems. He has contributed to the coming of the true light, which we all feel is dawning, as much as any other man. His single tax would be a great advance in the right direction if it could be put in operation. In fact, it would put the burden of government upon those who as things are now constituted have the greatest advantage, as he has demonstrated—*i. e.*, the rent gatherers. Nor would this be any disadvantage to our farmers, as the concealing of their personal property by capitalists and the tariff, which works directly against them, make the present system much more burdensome to them than the single tax would be; provided, always, that the amount so raised would be only "sufficient for the support of government economically administered."

This single tax would go far toward giving all an equal start in the race of life, just as the horse-racers equalize their steeds by the adjustment of their weights.

This is in accord with the scriptural rule: "Of him that hath much, much will be required."

If we could have a land tax and a tax graded on incomes, we would have this principle put into almost perfect operation. This would interfere with no property rights, and introduce no violent alienation in the realm of politics.

CHAPTER IV.
THE REVOLUTION PROPOSED IN SOCIALISM.

LET us first get some idea of the revolution which socialism proposes to bring about. As clear a statement of it as I know is the following, made by Professor Ely in his "Introduction to Political Economy:"

Socialism means coercive co-operation not merely for undertakings of a monopolistic nature, but for all productive enterprises. Socialists seek the establishment of industrial democracy through the instrumentality of the State, which they hold to be the only way whereby it can be obtained. Socialism contemplates an expansion of the business functions of government until all business is absorbed. All business is then to be regulated by the people in their organic capacity, each man and each woman having the same rights which any other man or any other woman has. Our political organization is to become an economical industrial organization, controlled by universal suffrage. Socialism will make civil service employees of all citizens, and will remunerate them in such manner as shall, in view of all the circumstances, appear to the public authorities to be just. Private property in profit-producing capital and rent-producing land is to be abolished, and private property in income is to be retained, but with this restriction: that it shall not be employed in productive enterprises. What is desired, then, is not, as is supposed by the uninformed, a division of property, but a concentration of property. The socialists do not complain because productive property is too much concentrated, but because it is not sufficiently concentrated. Socialists consequently rejoice in the formation of trusts and combinations, holding that they are a development in the right direction.

There are four elements in socialism, namely: First, the common ownership of the means of production; second, the common management of the means of production; third, the distribution of the annual products of industry by common authority; fourth, private property in income. Socialists make no war upon capital, strictly speaking. No one but a fool could do such a thing. What socialists object to is not capital, but the private capitalist. They desire to nationalize capital, and to abolish capitalists as a distinct class by making everybody, as a member of the community, a capitalist—that is, a partial owner of all the capital in the country.

It ought not to be hard to picture socialism to one's self. Government owns the post-office; most governments own the telegraph; nearly all own the wagon roads; some own the canals and railways; many governments own factories; probably every national government does at least a little manufacturing; most governments cultivate forests, and some cultivate more or less land. We have only to imagine an extension of what already exists, until government cultivates all land, manufactures all goods, conducts all exchanges, and carries on, in short, every productive enterprise—and we have socialism, pure and simple. (Pp. 240-242.)

Mr. Bellamy's "Looking Backward" is a fanciful and interesting presentation of the hopes, as well as the principles, of socialism. Socialism is not a senseless cry for a part of existing wealth, but it is a philosophical arraignment of the present basis of distribution—a system remorselessly logical and based upon the accepted axioms of political economy. It is, too, in close sympathy with humanity's needs.

Yet I believe that careful scrutiny of its principles and purposes will discover that they are impracticable, unless we could first change the nature of man. I will give the reader the reasons which have led the writer to that conclusion.

As Mr. George's proposal partook largely of the nature of socialism, so every objection urged against his views is still more forcible against this farther stretch of the same principles. Leaving out the difficulty of inaugurating this revolution (for it is evident that it will only come when the present order of things becomes unendurable), I will confine my objections to the system as it would be if once fully inaugurated.

And, first, there is the same old difficulty of committing so much power to the hands of the government. This is no chimera of the brain, conjured up to frighten the unthinking; it is real. The world has never yet seen the government pure, disinterested, honest, impartial, and capable enough to manage the vast trust that would be confided to them. The army of supervisors would have almost unlimited power to continue themselves in office. The party in power could take measures to intrench themselves in power until it would become almost impossible to ever dislodge them. Inch by inch there would grow up a governing class, distinct from all others and assuming a superiority to all others; and inch by inch this class would obtain advantages, until the great body of the people would become their vassals.

But the great trouble comes from the fact that the mass of the people would not be prepared for the sudden change in their condition. These would be of two kinds. Those from whom property had been taken in this sudden change would be one. While these might not deserve much pity, as they would not be deprived of any thing but the useless luxuries of life, yet they would constitute a vast dissatisfied element in the body politic—always a serious thing in a government. The second class would be something much more serious. They would consist of those who from the lowest condition would suddenly be placed in as good a condition as any other man. Even if this was not a condition of great luxury, it would be a vast change to them; vaster than at first glance it might appear; for conditions are relative, and as these would have come from the lowest condition, where vast multitudes were in advance of them, and had now reached a point where they were in as good a condition as any, it would be a rise enough to turn the head of even the well-educated and the conservative. But these would be neither the one nor the other: they would be ignorant, many of them vicious and depraved. The results of this sudden change would be morally disastrous in the extreme. Have you noticed the result of the sudden rise in worldly prosperity upon character? In how few instances was it beneficial? In how many instances was it disastrous? Now try this experiment upon a world-wide scale, and the result must be something terrible to contemplate. How many of this vast band would simply take the improved condition as a vantage-ground to indulge vices which before lay beyond their reach? Are we told that this change of condition will extirpate these vices? We were once told the same in regard to education. It has not proved true in that case; neither will it prove true in this case. Improvement in the condition of man, without a corresponding improvement in his moral *status*, is of little advantage to him or to society; in fact, in the majority of cases it is positively hurtful. This is not a re-assuring view of humanity, but nothing is gained toward solving our problem by leaving out the most important factor in it. It may facilitate the reaching of an apparent solution, but it will insure its being an erroneous one.

This tendency of which we have just spoken is in addition to the pauper spirit, and it reaches a larger number than the last, but it leaves the pauper spirit to flourish in this rich soil. The pauper spirit is the desire to live off the world without giving an equivalent in work or money. It says: "The world owes me a living." Now as society, in this new arrangement, would be organized on this very principle; and as there would be provisions made to support the indigent, it would all result in the nurture and increase of this unfortunate, helpless, and dangerous class. Of course there would be efforts made to circumvent them, but our tramp genus is very fertile in expedients; he is a camp follower, and it will be found hard to make him do his part in the industrial army.

Nor is it only in reference to these classes that socialism would have an unfortunate effect upon character. All who have studied man, and the influences that help and hinder in the formation of his character, must see that this interference with liberty on one side, and this dependence upon government, would destroy individuality.

After all, unless there was a *radical change in man's nature as well as his condition, there would remain in the world after these changes as much of sin, vice, crime, dissatisfaction, and trouble as there now is. All these revolutions but turn the patient over on his sound side; yet the knots in his hard bed, which will make another sore spot even worse, are not removed. The whole effort to devise a patent-right adjustment of mankind that will do away with all trouble and friction, while the natures of the parties remain unchanged, must ever end in failure.

The problem is too difficult, the factors entering into it too many, and too many of them are unknown, for any human intellect to master beforehand the result.

The difficulty we incur in each of these movements is human wickedness. Now this is precisely what causes the trouble in the present order of things. If it were not for wickedness, the earth might be rendered a paradise under almost any government, or with almost any system of property holding; and so long as wickedness survives we are going to have trouble and friction.

Nevertheless, the agitation of these reforms has done good. It shows us more clearly what is the chief difficulty in the way of human progress, no matter along what road we propose to advance. These difficulties may be generalized as wickedness.

Again, they present to us a goal of universal helpfulness and brotherly love, toward which we are urged to make our way. This must have an uplift to it.

Then the dissatisfaction with present things, so far as they are hurtful, and the active effort to better them, are hopeful and helpful in themselves. When dealing with the individual sinner, we always consider him in a hopeful state when he feels the guilt and helplessness of his condition. He is then in the proper state of mind to fly to a Saviour. So, when I find the world awake to the fact that it needs something, and that it needs it bad, I conclude that the world is getting in the state of mind to accept in earnest her only hope of real salvation from her difficulties: the application of the principles of Christ to the practical affairs of life.

CHAPTER V.
CHRISTIANITY OR SOCIALISM.

WHILE the writer sees the objections to socialism, which have been urged, and others which it is not necessary to present here; still I believe that it must be either socialism or Christianity actually put to practice which is to be the final social revolution among men. These two are mutually exclusive, and between them they cover the whole field, leaving no room for any other theory.

If Christianity be not true, and we take the principles of materialistic economists as true, and build our right to property upon the basis of personal labor alone, then we are forced to the conclusion that property is unjustly distributed. On this basis we cannot defend the right to land, or of monopoly, or of bequest, and only to a limited extent of inheritance. In fact, the right to the greater part of the immense fortunes of our day would be swept away.

Socialism and Christianity alike declare the solidarity of the human race and the brotherhood of man. Alike, too, they declare that all things belong to the race and not the individual. Socialism makes the race take charge of its estate through government. And socialism endeavors to equalize the condition of men.

Christianity is essentially a system dealing with individuals, and holding them to a strict account. Christianity says that all things belong to God, and that he bestows them upon men. It is a system of individualism; but it makes each individual God's direct agent to work for the good of men, of the race.

Now if we reject socialism and claim property under title from God, then we must take that title with the limitations God has put upon it. This makes you a mere trustee to use that property for the good of the race. This puts the responsibility for the right use of property upon every one to whom he has committed any of this world's goods.

If we reject Christianity, there is no logical basis for the defense of property rights as now existing. If we accept Christianity, and claim our property under its principles, then we are self-convicted of unfairness if we simply use that for our own pleasure which was committed to us in trust for the race. To be honest we must hold this property as a sacred trust, and subject to all the regulations of Him from whom it is derived.

Let me illustrate this position of the rich of our day: We will suppose that A is a rich Western farmer, who has several farms. B is an acquaintance of his from the older States, who comes to him without means. A rents B a farm in a neighboring county, A furnishing the teams, provisions for man and beast, farm utensils, seeds, and every thing needed to make a crop. B and his boys furnish the labor, and the two are to divide the crops equally. B is put in possession of the farm, and months go by. At last A concludes to visit B, to see how prospects for harvest are. He drives over; and when he gets in the neighborhood, he is surprised to find the fields all lying fallow, and not a sign of a crop, or of any work being done. He calls at the house; and Mrs. B, dressed expensively and handsomely, meets him and conducts into a room elegantly furnished. A is bewildered. He knew that when the family came they had absolutely nothing. He inquires for B and the boys, and learns that they are off on a hunt. He asks why no crop has been planted, and learns that they found enough on the place to last them for a year or so, and hence it was not necessary for them to work. He learns that the teams and utensils have been sold to supply the expensive furniture which he sees around. In fact, he learns that his old friend has been treating every thing as if it belonged to himself. Do you suppose that A would stand such treatment? Well, that is precisely the way the rich man, who uses his wealth simply to gratify his own tastes, and to minister to his own pleasures, is treating God. Nor is it the Maker alone who is wronged. As we have seen, the race has an interest in that estate, which has been entirely ignored. No wonder the poor feel that the fair thing is not being done to them.

So, whichever position we take, we see that as things are now adjusted and managed they are not on a just basis. And all are beginning to feel this. When this is the case—when humanity feel and know that an injustice is existing, we may look for a change. If we change from the present order, it must, as we have shown, be in one of two directions: toward socialism or toward practical Christianity. If we take the route to socialism, we plunge into an experiment, and into the dark.

The only light lies toward Christ, where we will have the guidance of him not one of whose sayings or laws have been proved false or erroneous by nineteen centuries of experience. Here, however, is where we strike a very important question: What is applied Christianity? Is it the making of all that a man can by grinding his employees, by trampling under foot all mercy for those that work for him, and then giving away some trifles of his profits in promiscuous and careless charity? This does more harm than good. Is the smallness of the amounts given the cause of the failure? By no means. If these amounts were largely increased, it would result in harm rather than good. Count Tolstoi, in his book "What to Do?" tells of his efforts to distribute, after personal investigation in Rzhandoff house, the very lowest quarter in Moscow, to the necessities of the occupants, of the fact that there was much less distress than he expected, and of his utter failure to do any good. He took many names of those who wanted help, and here is what he says of the result: "I will mention here that, out of all these persons whom I noted down, I really did not help a single one, in spite of the fact that for some of them that was done which they desired, and that which, apparently, might have raised them. Three of their number were particularly well known to me. All three, after repeated rises and falls, are now in precisely the same situation that they were in three years ago."

He was a good, conscientious man, trying with a large estate to do good. He came to the conclusion not only that he did no good, but that this careless giving was not good. He says: "I had gone so far astray that this taking of thousands from the poor with one hand, and this flinging of kopeks with the other, to those whom the whim moved me to give, I called good."

Nor is Tolstoi the only one who looks upon what is ordinarily called "charity" as a mistake.

I think that possibly this idea is carried too far. The day has not yet come when each of us is not called upon to do a good deal of this personal giving, and Christianity demands that we do this whenever necessary. But this merely palliates the disease of society in special and concrete cases. It is no remedy for the disease; and, carried too far, it augments the trouble.

Well, is it "applied Christianity" to turn over our spare means to the Church to manage for mankind? The Church is God's chosen vessel to bear to mankind the word of life, and the Church has a right to expect from those who have means all that she needs to accomplish her work. She can draw her checks upon men for houses in which to preach the gospel, for proper support for her ministers, for means by which to carry the gospel to the "earth's remotest bounds," and for the help of the afflicted; but it will interfere with her legitimate work for her to attempt too much. It is not her duty, nor a part of her legitimate work, for her to administer the surplus wealth of mankind for the common good. The solution of the question, then, is not in putting men's surplus into the hands of the Church. "It is not reason that we should leave the word of God to serve tables."

Christianity is essentially a system of individuals united together in a great co-operative society whose binding cord is love, in whose whole scheme the individual is thrown upon his own resources, and each individual is held to a strict account for the discharge of his duties. There are those now, as we have seen, who object to this system of individualism, and who want to substitute for it a system of communism, in which individual responsibility will be substituted by governmental responsibility. We have reviewed this proposal, and endeavored to point out the objections against it. Now let us examine the system of individualism, which God seems to have chosen by his Providence in the world's history, as well as in his Word. It has been attacked as totally inadequate to meet the needs of the great aggregations of men incident to the developments of modern times. Will these objections hold when subjected to close scrutiny? Are the disadvantages of individualism offset by advantages that can be found in another system?

In this inquiry it is necessary for us to keep in view the end which we hope to reach by our system. An examination of the plans of communists shows that they propose to increase the amount of material goods held by each individual of the masses, and they presume that such increase of possessions will improve the character of the individual himself. On the other hand, Christianity, as the system that God has chosen for man, proposes as its chief aim to improve the character of each man, and leave him with his aroused manhood and quickened energies to improve his own material condition. The bare statement of the ends proposed by each system, and of the philosophy upon which they are constructed, seems to me to display the tremendous advantage of the divinely chosen one over the proposed improvement by man. God has revealed that "a man's life consisteth not in the abundance of the things which he possesseth." It is the "life" which God values, and not its environment; and it is this which is the real valuable quality among men. That system, then, which best deters and restrains man from the courses that degrade and destroy his life, and which best impels and stimulates him to develop and improve, is the system best adapted to man in his present condition. This is precisely, as I claim, what individualism does.

In the present order of things man is deterred from evil courses because those courses lead quickly to personal suffering and distress. This is true of all; but, as a law, it presses with varying force upon different classes of men. Those who have property are able to postpone the financial and social effects of dissipation much longer than the poor man. But this advantage is offset by the greater physical and moral ravages wrought in the individual himself. Adam Smith, the father of political economy, noticed the operation of these punishments fixed in the nature of things, not only to deter from evil courses the common people, but to act as a help to their consciences to raise the standard of right living; and he also notices the relaxation of these punishments in the case of the upper classes. We have only to substitute the words "poor" and "rich" for the terms of equal import in his argument to make all he says applicable to our time and country. In the discussion of the subject of a State Church, he says:

> In every civilized society, in every society where the distinction of ranks has once been completely established, there have been always two different schemes or systems of morality cur-

rent at the same time; of which the one may be called the strict or austere, the other the liberal or, if you will, the loose system. The former is generally admired and revered by the common people; the latter is commonly more esteemed or adopted by what are called people of fashion. The degree of disapprobation with which we ought to mark the vices of levity, the vices which are apt to arise from great prosperity and from the excess of gayety and good-humor, seems to constitute the principal distinction between those two opposite schemes or systems. In the liberal or loose system luxury, wanton and even disorderly mirth, the pursuit of pleasure to some degree of intemperance, the breach of chastity, at least in one of the two sexes, etc., provided they are not accompanied with gross indecency, and do not lead to falsehood or injustice, are generally treated with a good deal of indulgence, and are easily either excused or pardoned altogether. In the austere system, on the contrary, those excesses are regarded with the utmost abhorrence and detestation. The vices of levity are always ruinous to the common people; and a single week's thoughtlessness and dissipation is often sufficient to undo a poor workman forever, and to drive him through despair upon committing the most enormous crimes. The wiser and better sort of the common people, therefore, have always the utmost abhorrence and detestation of such excesses, which, their experience tells them are so immediately fatal to people of their condition. The disorder and extravagance of several years, on the contrary, will not always ruin a man of fashion; and people of that rank are very apt to consider the power of indulging in some degree of excess as one of the advantages of their fortune, and the liberty of doing so without censure or reproach as one of the privileges which belong to their station. In people of their own station, therefore, they regard such excesses with but a small degree of disapprobation, and censure them either very slightly or not at all. ("Wealth of Nations," p. 624.)

This shows a clear discernment of the effect of the present scheme of things upon men's characters and upon their material welfare; a discernment far in advance of those philosophers of our day who insist that poverty produces crime, and who think to remove vice from among men by putting it in their power to indulge in it. And is not much of the envy of the rich, and much of the anxious longing to so change the present order as to make us all on an equality, all practically wealthy, the outcome of a belief that considers "the power of indulging in some degree of excess, . . . and the liberty of doing so without censure or reproach," as one of the most desirable of earthly things? But what thinker does not see that this is not to be desired at all? The Psalmist saw of old that the disadvantage of the rich was that "their feet were set in slippery places," their position involved extra moral risks. Yet it is the very disadvantage of riches, perhaps, which is most longed for. And it is one of the chief advantages which poverty offers to humanity, the wall which it raises against vice, that constitutes the very ground of the fight that many make against it. There is a poverty, to be sure, that is a mother to crime. This is that state of utter wretchedness in which all individual dignity, worth, and character are lost in a mass of utter ruin, which we call the criminal classes. This is that awful slough of misery, that hell on earth, which is itself the effect of wickedness, toward which the wicked of all classes are surely slipping, in which all the lineaments of manhood are eliminated from humanity, and only the beast survives. This hell can only be filled up by removing the wickedness that has dug it. Nor is it more of a curse than of a pest-house in which the morally infected of the race are confined.

Not only does the present order of things deter from vice, but it offers the most splendid prizes to the individual as a reward for personal effort and worthiness. And here the position of honorable poverty, being most advantageous for the formation of character, has greatly the advantage over wealth as a point from which to start to win all the greatest prizes that are offered to man in this world. This is fair, too; for the disadvantage of poverty in its greater liability to drop immediately into a state of wretchedness has already been noticed. In this way the relative advantages of each class in society have been equalized. It is not necessary for me to prove to any man of observation that it is a real advantage to be a poor man if a man proposes to work for any of the noblest and best premiums which society offers to true worth. Nor is great wealth absent from among these prizes. How many instances might each of us present from our own knowledge of individuals who have made their way from the most disadvantageous position to the ownership of large fortune and commanding influence! I remember one instance of one of the richest men in Texas who started life as a day laborer at fifty cents a day, and who made with his own hands the furniture he and his wife commenced housekeeping on. When I came to Dallas, Tex., in 1875, one of the most unique characters of that Western town was a man of middle age with a basket of cakes on his arm, who went up and down the streets, crying in a peculiarly shrill voice: "Nice cream cakes, one for a nickel, two for a dime." I have watched this gentleman (for he is a gentleman) rise in the world with astonishment and pleasure. I saw him get a bakery, then a store, then large amounts of real estate, then a factory; and then his name began to appear on all sorts of bank and manufacturing boards, and at the head of most of the great enterprises of the city. Such instances as these two show the possibility before every enterprising young man, however poor he may be. Who can estimate the impetus that the example of such success gives to the thousands of struggling workmen, and the aggregate effect of their efforts in pushing forward the car of civilization? But wealth is the smallest and the least probable prize that the world holds out to the industrious young man. All the prizes of scholarship, of oratory, of political power, of military glory, of ecclesiastical usefulness and prominence, of benevolent enterprise, and of professional success, are more readily in the grasp of the poor than the rich. Yet none of these splendid prizes lie beyond the reach of either class. All who have the native endowment, which nature distributes impartially, and who will exercise the industry and self-denial necessary, may reach the point of excellence and of success. And he who has no chance to master adverse fate, who is compelled to labor under the burdens of poverty and obscurity all his days, has yet in his grasp the very highest prize that can be drawn: that of moral excellence. There are no circumstances where man cannot maintain his integrity; and the greater the difficulties under which he labors, and the mightier the obstacles he overcomes, the nobler the virtue which is the product of the struggle.

Now if we extend these lines of man's decline as the result of sin until they end in a real hell, and the line of his exaltation as the reward of virtue until it ends at the throne of God, we will have the scheme of our world as outlined in the Bible. If we keep our eye fixed upon the fact that character is the chief thing had in view, we are compelled to believe that this scheme is the best possible for man in his present condition. As man advances out of his present moral night, he will more and more come under the influence of that love and all the principles which Christianity advocates, and which will bind the race in closer and closer bonds of mutual co-operation and helpfulness; so that we will find a state where all the advantages of communism are found in combination with all the advantages of individualism. We will thus have industrial democracy in its best form.

PART IV.

WHAT CAN WE DO TO PROMOTE REFORMATION IN MONEY MATTERS?

CHAPTER I.

WHAT CAN INDIVIDUALS DO?

WE have seen the imminence of revolution in the methods of property-holding and distribution, and we have seen the necessity for reformation. We have already discussed the various schemes of revolution proposed by various classes of thinkers, and have tried to point out the reasons why they do not meet the case; and we have come to the conclusion that "applied Christianity" is the only remedy, and we have seen somewhat what is not "applied Christianity." It remains to inquire if there is any thing that can be done at present, besides the effort to spread Christianity over the world, to improve our condition. What can the individual member of society, anxious to see things upon a more equitable basis, do to bring about a better state?

1. What can a poor man who is a Christian do? There are few of us who are in a more favorable position to lend a hand to aid in bringing about a better condition of things. Let not such a one suppose that he is too insignificant to have any influence for good. He ought to be a potent factor. He should endeavor to square his own life by the principles set forth in Part II., and so put his influence on the right side of things. Especially is it necessary for him to realize that moral good and not wealth, character and not happiness, is the chief thing to be valued. Then he ought to remember what is said about contentment. He should not allow any prejudice to arise between

him and any class of his fellow-citizens. Especially he should not allow any of these things to make him feel out of place in the Church of God, or to get out of harmony with it in his feelings. Leave Him to whom vengeance belongs, and who is the judge of all men, to deal with recreant children. Let him put forth all his strength to raise his family and to imbue his comrades with the principles of Christianity. Our poor Christians have as much right in the Church of Christ as our millionaires, and they should feel this way about it. They should not permit the rich, even if they wanted to (and I have seen but little evidence that they do), to drive them from their place in the kingdom of our common Lord. They should attend services, dressed neatly and cleanly, and should make themselves at home there. They should not demand any petting or help. They should be independent and manly, respecting themselves, and they will command the respect and the love of their brethren. I have never been pastor where some of the poor of the Church did not command as much respect, and their voice was not as influential, as the average member. Brethren in humble circumstances, the future depends upon the prevalence of Christianity, and the success of Christianity depends largely upon you. Do not let the false cry of "Lo, here!" or "Lo, there is a saviour!" deceive you. Christ is our hope. Do not allow any one to throw your influence against the Church. Remember that in all your walk you have to maintain the respectability and the amiability of Christianity.

2. What can a poor man who is not a Christian do? He can become a Christian, of course; and in this

way not only help forward the reform, but save his own soul. But if he does not take such a step, he can recognize Christianity as an ally, and not an enemy. If he will so treat her, it will be an immense addition to the strength of the Church and of the poor men of our nation. But the only complete remedy is complete identification of interests by becoming a member of the Church. The mightiest enginery on earth can be readily captured by the poor man, and used legitimately to advance his influence, if he does not let some foolish man persuade him that some popgun of man's devising is a more effective instrument. Membership in the Church will do a great deal for any poor man, as Adam Smith points out. One of the great difficulties of the laborers of our day is that the individual is lost in a mass where his conduct is neither observed nor cared about by the public. In such circumstances he is apt to think that there is no matter what he does. In other words, he is in danger of losing the mighty restraining influence of public opinion. Now if the individual laborer becomes a member of the Church—not nominally, but really—taking an interest in all her services and becoming identified with her work, by this very fact he has emerged from the general mass; he has individualized himself. Henceforth the eyes of his fellow-members are on him, and so are the eyes of all his associates who learn of his profession; so that he is immediately surrounded by that pressure of public opinion which is beneficial to men in all classes and conditions. Individual dignity and individual worthiness are what our workmen need more than organization. The addition of cyphers produces nothing but cyphers. Each workman has it in his power to make himself a force in the body politic. The great ingredient in this, however, is moral worth. I do not mean to say a word against the combination of workmen in societies intended to advance their mutual interests and to improve their membership. Such societies are good; they give a public opinion, the necessity of which I have spoken. The society becomes interested in the public conduct of each of its members, and will exercise a good influence over him. Then the debates, etc., incident to their meetings will stimulate his thinking and help to develop him. Then the direct influence of these societies upon employers will generally be good and not evil.

I am especially anxious that there be no antagonism between the workmen of our nation and the Church. Their interests are one; they are mutually dependent, and have only good and not evil to expect from each other. It will indeed be the height of folly for them to allow their forces to be divided in this fight for the rights of humanity. The Church is the only power on earth which can mediate between the poor and the rich. At her altars they both meet. She can lay her hands upon both sides of the controversy, and can authoritatively declare to each the commands of God. And the solution of our difficulties depends upon both sides of the controversy uniting in some agreement that will be equally advantageous and honorable. There is nothing to be hoped for in the direction of either of these classes conquering the other and destroying it. That would be humanity's loss, and not gain. The Church may not be doing all that she ought, and many think that she ought to do things which lie beyond her province. For a discussion of her part in this great work I refer you to the last chapter of this book. All I am after here is to prevent, as far as I may be able, the attempt to divorce the Church of God and the laboring-man. They are allies, not enemies.

3. What can a rich man, who is a Christian, do? Upon him, at the present juncture, rests the heaviest responsibility of all. It is to him we must look largely to prove to the world that our religion is more than a name. He it is who can show that Christianity is adapted to the solution of all the problems of our civilization, is the product of a wisdom far above the capacity of man, of a wisdom that "sees the end from the beginning." And what ought he to do? Live like a Christian, that is all. But his Christianity must enter into all his business and all his relationships. We refer him to the principles laid down in Part II., and call on him to embody them in his life. We have already said that it is not necessary to stop making money, or to give all his money away. I now say that if his talent is that of an organizer of legitimate enterprises, if he can prepare the way for the profitable employment of large numbers of men, then that talent is not only a rare one, but one of the most useful among men. He would do a great wrong to let such a talent lie idle. But let him remember that it is the employment of the men and thus furnishing them the opportunity to make a good living for themselves and families, a far better thing than supporting them directly by his charity, which makes his a great work, and not the profit he can contrive to make out of the enterprise for him-

self. Let him remember that every one of his employees is a brother, is to be loved as a brother, and to be treated as one. Let every Christian employer, from the lady with one servant up, remember that their employees are human, are brethren, and establish as cordial as possible relations with them. It is through the heart that we reach mankind. A kind word of personal interest spoken will do far more than some real favor bestowed upon a person as a sense of duty, toward winning their love.

Right here in this bridgeless chasm, which has been dug between the employer and the employee, is the chief trouble that faces us. And I do not hesitate to say, that our old Southern slavery, for which the world has so abused us, where it took on its kindlier phases, with its cordial love between master and slave, with the slave a part of the very family life, was nearer the right Christian relation than any thing now existing in our country. Nothing can be worse than indifference but hate, and indifference will soon become hate. This treatment of all who work for you as though they were machines without feeling and without souls is a crying sin and shame. "On what meat has this our Cæsar fed that he has grown so great?" You, as a Christian, must get off your stilts and manifest a brother's interest in your brother, though he does happen to serve you. That does not prove that you are his superior. And let me say right here that nothing can be done, unless we can find some common platform where we cannot only meet but love one another, but rush right on in the way we are going, and which is leading to swift social destruction.

As things are now, a Christian employer seems to look upon his workmen as so many machines to help him make money for himself and family, and to give to the rest of mankind and the Church. This ought to be exactly reversed. His first interest, after his own family, should be those who work under him.

It is difficult to present the abstract description of what Christian men should be, and what they should do with their wealth. But there is a concrete case at hand who has lived in our day, and who so nearly fulfills my highest ideal of the rich Christian man, that I beg leave to present an account of him found in the July number of the *Homiletic Review*, 1890. The subject of the article is the celebrated merchant, Mr. Samuel Morley, and the writer, Dr. J. M. Ludlow:

> Mr. Morley was a man of vast business capacity. Much of this he inherited, as he inherited the business itself. He was able to manage a manufacturing enterprise that gave employment to fully eight thousand persons, involving an almost infinite amount of details, as represented by a single mail delivery of over two thousand letters, and to make this gigantic and intricate machine run without a jar. The business was conducted upon the highest principles not only of finance, but of morals, so that his name became the synonym of mercantile honor. . . . Samuel Morley was also a leader in English charities. Just after his death, the Prince of Wales said in a public speech: "He will go down to posterity as one of the greatest philanthropists of the age." The extent of his money donations to charitable projects will never be known. Certainly he was the largest individual giver in England. He did not concentrate his benefactions as Peabody did, but scattered them with the thousand calls of daily needs. Among his papers are great stacks of begging letters marked with amounts he directed his secretary to send in response, ranging from $50 to $30,000 in single donations. And yet there was no giving at hap-hazard. Every case was searched out with as much care as if it had been a request

for credit in business. He doled nothing; but took an intense delight in watching the happiness he created, as we imagine the all-good Creator delights in the flowers that bloom on the dull earth. . . . He once offered a school prize for the best essay. A little fellow of ten years ambitiously competed for it, but was unsuccessful. Mr. Morley sent him a gift of equal value for having tried so hard. The boy was Charles Spurgeon, and the event was the first knitting of the chord of affection that lasted for life between the greatest of preachers and the greatest of merchants. . . . .

Prominent were his religious donations. He was a great dissenter, a thorough believer in the independent system of Churches. He endowed the colleges of his denomination, pushed all schemes for its evangelistic work at home and abroad. Poor Churches were sustained, half-paid ministers made comfortable, and mission chapels planted among the destitute.

It was the writer's happiness to be thrown with Mr. Morley as a fellow-passenger across the Atlantic. He had a remarkable power of winning even strangers to him, and was seldom seen without a group of persons about him. Though there were clergymen on board, Morley must lead the Sunday evening meeting, giving out the hymns, singing them heartily, and making a happy little talk, that caught the heart-strings of everybody—Jew, infidel, and Christian of every sort.

Another of Mr. Morley's hobbies was that of political reform, especially such as aimed at the liberties of the common man. As early as 1843, though a young man, he threw himself heart and soul into the agitation for the repeal of the corn laws, the enormous tax upon foreign grain importations that kept the working-man in an almost starving condition, the repeal of which made England a market for our great Western prairies, enriching both countries. In this young Morley stood shoulder to shoulder with Richard Cobden and John Bright. He was President of the Administrative Reform Association, or Civil Service League, with such men to help him as Layard, Charles Napier, Charles Dickens, which, after fifteen years, succeeded in getting open competitive examinations instead of secret patronage of government officers, and in breaking up the habit of purchasing rank in the army, leaving such honors to be won on the field or in military council. . . . .

What Can Individuals Do? 155

As his wealth increased, he felt more and more his brotherhood with the poor man. He adopted a pension system for the workmen as they were disabled through years. He visited these worthy fellows, took them by the hand, and left something substantial in it. In no year did he distribute less than ten thousand dollars pension money in his own factories. He never discharged his faithful men. If trade was dull, their hours were shortened. When trade was brisk, they had not the face to strike. His factories contained not only work-rooms, but library, reading-room, parlor, and all the ordinary conveniences of a respectable club-house. The buildings were always models of cleanliness, light, ventilation, for he held himself responsible for the health and good cheer of every one of the thousands he employed.

The house of Morley always paid the highest wages, was the first to lead in an advance, and always the last to order a reduction. His care of his men was not left merely to a good system. He paid the salaries of his clerks with his own hand, that he might look every one of them in the face and have a word with each that would establish a sort of kinship—that kindness which is more than kin. There was no man to whom the humblest would go more quickly if in trouble than to the boss; and, if necessary, the boss would go to the man's home. He took a pride in having all well housed. The village where he lived he changed from a tumbled-down nest of houses into one of the prettiest home neighborhoods in England; reconstructing the cottages, planting trees, laying out gardens, offering prizes for the best kept places, and supplying gratuitously all shrubbery from his own nursery, building a beautiful chapel [undenominational], his motto being, "Think and let think," though he had very decided convictions about dogma himself. Mr. Morley looked beyond his own employees, and was the great patron of the Society, to help every man to a home, which erected on easy terms nearly five thousand cottages of the most improved sanitary model. He threw himself purse and heart into the Agricultural Union. In 1874 a farm laborer could not earn more than nine shillings, about $2.25, a week, with sixpence a day for a child to act as scarecrow. By this association wages were doubled. His motto was for every man fair wages, a cottage, and a garden. How his blood tingled with shame and wrath when he read the words of a certain political economist classing the plow and the plowman together as commodities to be bought! In the public newspapers Morley, the capitalist, denounced the idea, and wrote words as strong in behalf of the dignity of the laborer as Henry George could have penned. He offered his pen, his tongue, his vote in Parliament to the cause. If labor candidates needed funds to secure their fair canvass in any election, his purse was theirs for the campaign.

In this noble man we have almost the exact embodiment of my idea of what a rich man ought to do for his race. Whether all his methods were wise or not does not affect the question; his spirit was right, and his intentions good. The popularity of such men as he and our own Peter Cooper with the working-classes while they lived, and the mourning for them when dead, shows that such a recognition of them as fellow-men, such an effort to do their duty to the workmen, broke down entirely the wall between the classes of which we hear. If our rich would follow their example, the hearts of the poor would be completely captured by them.

4. What can a rich man who is not a Christian do? I will include in this inquiry not only the openly ungodly, but also the vast number of nominal Christians who are in all our Churches from the ranks of wealth. Of course the best possible step would be to become genuine Christians, and let the principles of Christianity rule their lives. Merely being connected with some Church or simply patronizing religion will not do. There has been too much of that sort of religion among them which Thackeray satirized when he represented the attitude of the upper classes to Christianity as reminding him of a committee of lords of some charity hospital tasting soup upon some public

occasion with an air that said: "This is excellent soup, for paupers." Religion don't need your patronage; nor does the poor man need religion any more than you do; nor is there one standard of morals for the poor, and another for you.

But whether the rich man accepts religion or not, he can accept and act upon that idea of property which Christianity presents. This is the only defensible position for him to take. If he rejects this, he cuts the very basis from under himself. But it is manifestly unfair for him to accept these principles so far as they affect his title to property, and then reject them in the control of the property which they confer on him. Now if the wealthy classes will just begin to acknowledge their trusteeship, and to use their surplus in some way for the general good, it will be a long step in the right direction. Such a step would extinguish the fuse to the bombs that threaten to blow up all their rights.

A public sentiment among the wealthy, that a man must do something for the race or disgrace himself, would result in converting many a society dude into a man. And such a sentiment would be strictly just. The man who has a surplus and will not give it to benefit mankind is an embezzler of trust money, and would be treated right if society so regarded him. "Society" thus could be a mighty help, and it would be an act of self-preservation.

CHAPTER II.
What Can and Should the State Do?

THE State is God's instrument in this world for the accomplishment of a certain purpose. Paul, in Romans xiii. 1–7, clearly reveals our relation to the government, and the government's relation to God. He speaks with divine authority, saying: "Let every soul be subject unto the higher powers. For there is no power but of God: the powers that be are ordained of God. Whosoever therefore resisteth the power, resisteth the ordinance of God: and they that resist shall receive to themselves damnation. For rulers are not a terror to good works, but to the evil. Wilt thou then not be afraid of the power? do that which is good, and thou shalt have praise of the same: for he is the minister of God to thee for good. But if thou do that which is evil, be afraid; for he beareth not the sword in vain: for he is the minister of God, a revenger to execute wrath upon him that doeth evil. Wherefore ye must needs be subject, not only for wrath, but also for conscience sake. For, for this cause pay ye tribute also: for they are God's ministers, attending continually upon this very thing. Render therefore to all their dues: tribute to whom tribute is due; custom to whom custom; fear to whom fear; honor to whom honor."

Here then we have it, "the powers that be are ordained of God," and "they are God's ministers." Further, the laws of government, constituted by proper authority, become the laws of God, and disobedience to them becomes sin; for, "Whosoever resisteth the power, resisteth the ordinance of God: and they that resist shall receive to themselves damnation." What a tremendous authority this gives to human enactments! And all these things are said of government at its worst, that of Nero in Rome. Nor is this remarkable passage merely an exhortation to the Christians to be submissive to authority, but it bases such submission on the absolute statements made here of the divine authority of all government. This position Peter also presents in 1 Peter ii. 13, 14. The Saviour himself, at the very time he was about to suffer death by an unjust decree of a judge, says: "Thou couldest have no power at all against me, except it were given thee from above."

Government is as surely a divine institution as the Church; and not only the abstract institution of government, but the existing governments are divine institutions. Their laws, where they do not controvene the higher laws of God, are God's laws, and the violation of them brings upon man the divine condemnation. One of the very evils of our day is the irreverence of the masses for the laws of the land. They regard law merely as the enactments of legislators, their neighbors, no wiser or better than themselves, to be respected if the government has power to enforce the penalty of the violation, but having no sacredness. And does not the Legislature itself, and the courts which construe its statutes, take the same view as to the merely human origin and authority of government and its laws?

Nothing could give such authority to our laws as to

thus base them on the authority of God. It would lead to greater reverence for all law on the part of the people, and it would prevent so much hasty legislation. In this view of the subject, government is God's instrument, and the Bible is as much the guide book of the statesman as of the preacher. This is not to unite Church and State, except in the eyes of those who would dethrone God in the realm of nature as well as that of sociology. The Bible would thus become the very basis of government, ranking above Magna Charta or the Constitution. But this Bible would be interpreted by the State itself and not the Church. The Bible thus becomes the text-book for statesmanship, as well as theology. But the statesman does not have to kneel at the feet of the priest to inquire the meaning of the Word; he simply uses his common sense, subject to review by the great public.

What are the functions of government? becomes now a pertinent inquiry. The passages we have quoted show that one great branch of its work is to restrain evil doers. God has another instrument designed to make man better, to reach his heart and put therein the principles of love, so that he becomes a benevolent factor in society, and not a malevolent one. In the meantime, however, while this leaven is working, there is a mighty section of the human race under the domination of selfishness, and this section needs to be restrained from committing depredations upon one another, and upon all others. To restrain them from the commission of crime by punishing all criminal acts is one of the chief functions of the State.

When Christ, the head of the Church, was approached upon the subject of dividing an inheritance justly, he said: "Who made me a judge and a divider over you?" He thereby repudiated the attendance upon such secular matters as a part of his work or that of his Church. It is left, then, as a part of the work of the State.

"Render to Cæsar the things that are Cæsar's, and to God the things that are God's," leaves the two questions of tax and currency in the hands of the State as the proper agency to attend to them.

The Bible does not attempt to set up a model government. It does not, even in the case of the Church, do more than lay down great principles, which man was to apply to the changing circumstances of life. So we have for the State merely great principles, broad lines marked out, and all the *minutiæ* and details left to man.

The punishment and prevention of crime, the just settlement of differences, the management of the currency, and the method of securing a support for its necessary institutions, and all that these things naturally involve, are committed to this secular arm of the Almighty upon earth. How then can this divinely instituted State help on a reform in money matters?

1. The State should frankly acknowledge God as the source of its authority, and should hold his Word as the received basis of all its laws. What other basis is there for government to rest on that will command the assent of mankind; or, what is more important, will command man's respect and reverence? The *contrat social* is an exploded hypothesis to which no thinker of our day pays any respect. And yet

much of the political reasoning of our time proceeds on the supposition that this myth is true philosophy. Such is the position of those who contend against the recognition of God or his Word by government. Others think that such a recognition of the Bible would constitute union between Church and State. Such, however, is not the fact, for the great majority of this nation believe in the Bible, and the various Churches claim it as the foundation of their doctrine, and but a small minority reject it. Yet these Churches are divided upon the interpretation of the same book. Now the State is not asked to accept some one Church's interpretation of this book, or to indorse any Church, or to forward the interests of any one organization; but to acknowledge in theory what is largely the fact—her indebtedness to the Word of God, and her dependence upon it. Then the State should adjust her laws to this Word of God. Then Church and State, God's two great agencies, would, with united voices, say to mankind: "Thou shalt not." Who does not know that the authority of each would be vastly augmented in this case? As it is, what wonder the enactments of the State are evaded without scruple by men, when the State itself annuls the divine law in reference to divorce and the Sabbath? If the law is simply some other men's ideas of what I ought to do, then man feels no hesitancy to evade it, if he finds occasion to do so, and it does not involve too much risk. But when law comes with divine authority, and the Church, which enforces this authority upon the conscience, tells us that in disobeying the law of the State we disobey God, then law is exalted to its true place, and man will treat it with

What Can and Should the State Do?

added reverence. But so long as the State itself puts aside ruthlessly the law of God, and goes so far as to legalize what it distinctly condemns, the Church cannot teach otherwise than that the conscience must be governed by the Bible, no matter what the statutes of the country may say. This confuses the conscience, and makes men doubtful of the authority of all law. It subtracts much from the force of the voice of both Church and State; these two, which ought to supplement and complement each other, are found in opposition, each weakening and destroying the influence of the other. Right here we find the source of the almost universal irreverence for law simply as law which is so greatly lamented among us. If a given course is greatly condemned or approved, it is not because it is or is not lawful, but entirely owing to the instruction of the conscience in sources independent of government. How great a loss this is to government it is hard to tell; it is incalculable. Yet we find government in its highest councils, and its highest courts, compelled to appeal for authority to this Word of God, which, when it does not suit its convenience, is so readily set aside.

This recognition of the Bible as the base of the authority and the laws of government would necessarily make it a text-book in our schools and colleges along with the Constitutions of the States and general government. Whether the work of education properly belongs to the Church or the State is a debatable question; but it is not debatable that education should involve moral as well as intellectual development; nor is it hardly debatable that morals are so dependent on religion as to be inseparable from it;

and it certainly lies beyond controversy that Christianity is the religion of this country. It seems to me that this recognition of the secular side of the Bible, and its relation to the State, independently of its purely theological contents, would give us the foundation for instruction in morals based upon it, and entirely unaffected by sectarian bias.

2. Government, as God's secular arm upon earth, should be like its Master, and have no respect to persons; should be without partiality. There should be no "class legislation." Not only the laws as framed should be impartial, but the execution of them should be without partiality. In the execution of our criminal laws the same character of offense should have the same character of punishment meted out to it, whether the offender be rich or poor. The drunken member of a club should not be sent home in a cab, and the poor man in the same condition hurried off in a police wagon to the lock-up. The game of poker among gentlemen should not be overlooked, and the negro "crap" players hauled up before the magistrate. Government should be careful in extending the limits of the law against any given kind of conduct; it should be sure that such conduct was a real crime against some individual of society, or against the well-being of society as a whole; but having outlawed the conduct, the law should be executed in high society as well as in low society. Nothing is more the cause of the characteristic uneasiness and disregard of laws of our day than this partiality in their administration.

Government ought also to protect the poor man's property against the rich man's fraud, as well as the rich man's property against the poor man's stealing. There are selfish and lawless men in each class that will get their neighbor's goods without an equivalent if they can. The law ought to restrain this selfishness, and to prevent it accomplishing its purpose, whether it be a combination of rich men to fleece the poor by raising prices upon some necessity, or of thieves to carry on horse stealing. Wherever there is an effort to get property without an equivalent of some sort, there is an effort to commit a crime. Against all such crimes laws should be enacted and executed. Not all trusts and combinations can be condemned as such unlawful concerns, for many of them conduct a legitimate business. It is not the "trust" that is criminal, but the effort to get property for nothing, and that whether it is done by one man or many combining together. And all such breakings of the eighth commandment should be classed and punished as equally infamous. If there is any difference, the rich banker who steals the savings of the poor committed to his keeping is a worse rogue than the sneak thief who steals the banker's overcoat. Yet the last is stealing and the first is embezzlement; and if the embezzlement is managed with enough skill, the criminal may still be found in good society. Such false distinctions should be done away with, and all thieves, big and little, put upon an equality.

3. The burdens of supporting government should be so adjusted as to be fair to all parties and classes.

It is not so easy a matter to determine what is fair as it appears at first glance. It is by no means simply assessing an *ad valorem* tax upon all. There are other burdens, besides the support of the State officers and institutions, that belong to society as a whole, and are to be taken into consideration. It seems to me that we have been thrown off the right track by overvaluing property and undervaluing man. The protection of man is the primary object of government; the protection of his property is merely incidental to this. Hence this secondary purpose of government is to be sacrificed to the first if they come in conflict. The government is as much interested in the welfare of the lowliest of her citizens as of the highest; and it is the government's interest that each individual be a contented, happy, and useful member of society. When the individual becomes otherwise, he is a burden to society. Society is compelled to take care of every one of its members. It endeavors to make each earn his own living. But in the case of the criminal and the pauper, some other way must be provided, and this way has always been very expensive. But there are members of society, as children, who cannot take care of themselves. These individuals can always be most cheaply and satisfactorially provided for by the heads of the families to which they naturally belong. That this is the duty of such a head of the family does not alter the fact that he is doing a public service in the discharge of his duty, and one which the public should take cognizance of; for when society has, without the intervention of any such agent, to support an individual, it is both very expensive and unsatisfactory; and especially in the case of children it is almost impossible to accomplish the desired end: the making them into good citizens. So we see that the burden of the proper support of his family by the *paterfamilias* ought to be put to his credit in the adjustment of the burdens of society.

To illustrate what I mean, let us take four individuals, A, B, C, and D. A has an income of $100,000, B of $10,000, C of $1,000, and D of $400, and let each family be composed of the man, the wife, and three children. Now the government is as much interested in one of these individuals as another. It is specially interested in the development of each of those children into a self-respecting and useful member of society. Now fix upon some per cent. as representing society's legitimate claim upon each income, including in the calculation the burden of the support of the family. Let us say, as a mere basis of our calculation, that the State takes half of each income, and out of this half it allows the support of the family, in that rank of society which it occupies, to be deducted. This will leave A with $50,000 undistributed, and $50,000 to go to society, including his own family. Surely $5,000 will be enough to allow each member of A's family for a support. This will make $25,000 to be deducted, leaving $25,000 due the government for its general support. B will be left in the undisturbed possession of $5,000, and required to contribute an equal amount to the State, less the support of his family. As we have supposed that the income of the first is ten times that of the next, we will also suppose that their legitimate support differs in the same ratio. This will give B $500 to supply the wants of each of his family, or $2,500 in all, leaving $2,500 due the State from his income. So, in the case of C, he will have $500 for himself, and then $500 for the government, less the support of his family. If we were to allow the same ratio for the support of C's family as in B's case, it would give them only $50 each for food, clothes, mental and moral culture, and all other legitimate items of a support. This is manifestly insufficient. In fact, I cannot see how he can support his family on less than the whole $500 allowed for that purpose plus the support of the State. But we will suppose that the State takes $25 of the amount, and leaves $475 for the family. C still has $500 to draw on in case of need, and then lay up something for a rainy day besides.

Now we come to the most difficult case: that of D, with his $400 a year. Using our same principle, we would put aside $200 for himself, and $200 for the government, less the support of his family. But $200 will not nearly support his family in the way to make them self-respecting and to give his children an opportunity to make good citizens. The cheapest food will cost them $150, and their clothing at least $150 more; so that the support of the family will take up all that is allowed for the claim of society and $100 besides. The other $100 is not too much to be held for cases of sickness, or other emergencies. So that the State should accept the right support of the family by D as a full discharge of his duty to society. If the State overburdens him, and makes it impossible to properly support this family, it will result in discouraging him and impairing his earning powers; hence he will drop to a lower income. It will also result in the family, compelled to live poorer than their neighbors, being dissatisfied and unhappy. They will lose self-respect. In this condition there is constant danger of the family as a whole, or some individuals of it, dropping into the pauper class, when society, instead of getting any thing out of them for the general support, will have to support them; or into the criminal class, where they would be both more expensive and more dangerous. Manifestly the cheapest and the best thing for society to do is to leave D to devote all his earnings to the decent support of his wife and children. This, of course, is true of all who command a less income than has been supposed in the case of D. This would lift the whole burden of the support of the general government off of the poor and put it on the rich. How different is this from the actual tax system of our nation? According to this system, our man D would have a burden of at least $60 to bear, resulting in so much tax on him, though the greater part of it would never reach the coffers of the government, which is all the worse for the poor man, and to the advantage of the capitalists.

Would this adjustment of the burdens of State so that the poor man would be left to support his family decently, and the burden of the support of the government be placed upon those strong enough to bear it, be a just arrangement? In my opinion it would be just, equitable, and politic.

We must not forget in the discussion of the equities here that the support of the family is to be counted in, since if the man does not support his family it is thrown upon the government at an added expense. But not only is the poor man bearing his part of the common burden of society in supplying the wants of his family. He has less need of the protection of government than the rich man. So long as a man's wealth is at a moderate sum, he can more or less look after it, and protect it himself. The police of the city do very little toward the protection of a poor man's property; but when a man becomes rich, he cannot keep his own eye on his goods, he becomes more and more dependent upon the police to protect his posessions. What would Wanamaker's immense establishment be worth to him if there were no government in Philadelphia for one day's time? The mob would gut it in a few hours. But the man in that city who owns simply a good home can make it too dangerous, in proportion to the booty to be obtained, for the mob to enter his door.

Again, there is more or less of "unearned increment" in the increase of all great fortunes—that is, of value resulting from the existence and growth of society and not from the labors of the individual; and this is true in other cases as well as in the well-known one of land. If a merchant deserves credit for winning the good-will of his fellow-men, it does not alter the fact that he owes his prosperity to the good-will of society. And now the growth of society will result in the growth of his trade and profits. Thus the growth of society as a whole, which is impossible except under a stable government, results in the increase of many values directly, as the result of this growth itself and not of any man's labor. But this wealth, added to the sum of things by the direct growth of society, is generally garnered by a few. I repeat, there is more or less of this unearned increment in all great fortunes. Society can rightly tax this heavily, for it is hers.

Hence we conclude that it would be equitable to

adjust the burdens of government so as to lighten the burden of the poor man and to increase the burden of the rich. How this had better be done I will leave it to the statesman to find out. It is for practical statemanship to work out the details.

4. The government should so modify the laws of inheritance and bequest as to stop the accumulation and perpetuation of vast fortunes in the hands of individuals. To this end bequest might be done away with entirely. I do not think that there should be any limit put upon the legitimate acquisitions of any one, or upon his right to control or to give away his property so long as he lives. But put it out of the hand of a man to perpetuate such vast possessions when he is dead. Then limit the amount a man may inherit, say to $1,000,000. And limit inheritance to children from parents, and parents from children, and do away with it in all cases of collateral relationship. What sense is there in the present law that thwarts the will of the great Tilden, deprives society at large of its just rights to that estate, and puts it in the hands of men who had nothing to do with its acquisition, and for whom the gatherer of this wealth cared little? These few changes would violate no natural right, would not infringe upon the right of private property, and yet they would stop the dangerous tendency of wealth to drift into the hands of a few favored individuals and families.

5. The function of government to suppress crime involves its prevention, and the greatest move government could make in that direction would be the prohibition of the liquor traffic. This would decrease crime and its expense, it would stop one of the great-

est leakages in the earnings of the poor, hence tend to equalize distribution of property, and it would increase the amount of wealth and also the productive capacity of man. At the same time it would not violate any personal right of man, for no man has a right to injure another or to injure society. As this traffic is sought to be destroyed because it is an injury to society, and as society has the right to suppress all that is injurious, if it is defended it must be on the ground that it is not injurious to the body politic. I have no time to enter into this argument now, but I will say that I have no more doubt of society, through the government, having the right to suppress this evil than I have of its right to punish the murderer. Then the wife and children have an inalienable right to the earnings of the husband and father, or so much as is needed for a support, and the government ought to see that this right is not taken away by the saloon-keeper.

CHAPTER III.

WHAT CAN AND OUGHT THE CHURCH TO DO?

THE Church is God's agency for saving men. He designs by means of the Church to reach the individual man and convert him from a selfish into a benevolent being. The Church is to propagate the doctrine of Christ, and to persuade men to accept him as their Saviour. The Church is to labor to present man with the right ethical standards, and to bring men's characters to correspond to these standards. She finds all her doctrines and moral standards in the Bible, and it is her duty to impress these upon the hearts and consciences of men. As the State is God's strong arm to prevent man from dropping into a lower level, so the Church is his arm to lift man to higher and nobler heights. The prime mission of one is to restrain man from evil, of the other to persuade men to do good. Each is necessary, and each is divinely instituted. Each depends upon the Bible, each is supplementary of the other, and each is independent of the other. The sphere of each is distinctly marked. The Church should attend to spiritual things and leave the management of secular affairs to the State. But the Church must lift her voice for the right, and against the wrong, however such a course may affect the State or the parties which control the State. But the extent of her responsibility is met when she bears witness to the truth. She must declare the right principles, but she is not to use the machinery of the Church to push any policy or doctrine into practical legislation in the State.

The members of the Church, however, including her ministers, have all the right of citizens, and they have the right to combine as citizens with one another and with other citizens, to accomplish any political object they may desire. They have forfeited no franchise in becoming Christians or preachers of the gospel. But in all this political work they must be sure to act in their capacity of citizenship, and not to drag the Church into the political arena. The temptation to grasp any machinery that will advance their object is great, and it has not always been resisted by ministers and Church-members as it should have been.

There has been an error equally prevalent on the other side. If men find ministers and members of the Churches laboring to advance any political project, they often jump to the conclusion that because such action would be wrong if taken by the Church in its organized capacity it is therefore wrong for those who constitute the Church to do this thing in their capacity of citizens. But such is by no means the fact.

To see what the Church ought to do in the present to help in monetary reforms it will be well to examine her work in the reforms of the past. The natural position of the Church is that of a conservative. Her book tells her: "The powers that be are ordained of God." Hence she is naturally set for the defense of the present existing order of things at any given time, until she is convinced both of the injustice of such order and that it is not the best that can be done at that time. Hence almost every reform has at some point in its development met the opposition of the Church. Hardly a reformer but what has attacked the Church under the mistaken notion that it was the great enemy of reform. Many reformers have started out from among the ranks of Christian ministers; and because they could not hurry the Church forward as rapidly as they wished to travel, have landed among her bitterest enemies. The Church is right to proceed slowly, to "prove all things; hold fast that which is good." She acts as a great breakwater to hold in check the restless passions of men who would often destroy what they have before providing something better, if they were not held in check by some such power.

Yet no reform in any age that has met the united opposition of the Church has ever succeeded. In every successful reform there has been a point reached where the principle involved in it is believed in by a great part of the Church, and enforced by a large portion of her ministry. When the reform reaches this stage of development, the Church as an organization is put in a very difficult position; the eager reformers, and those of her own members who have accepted their doctrine, are anxious for her not only to preach the right doctrine, but to use all her power to push the political movement to a successful issue. They often go so far as to try to force the Church to compel her members to unite in their efforts or be expelled from her membership. On the other hand, those who oppose the proposed reforms, and especially those of her members who side with them, resent every utterance from the pulpit or from Church assemblies that enforces the principle which they condemn, and they contend strenuously that the Church is going beyond its right limits, that she is invading the field of party politics, that the movement means the union of Church and State, and that liberty is about to be forever destroyed. To steer between these two factions, to hold by the truth and proclaim it as truth, and yet not be entangled in party politics, becomes very difficult indeed.

Not only has no reform that met the united opposition of the Church ever succeeded, but no reform that has secured the indorsement of the great mass of the Churches, and become the settled conviction of the ministers, has ever failed of eventual success. Then only do reforms gather that moral momentum that is needed to bring victory; then only is the conscience of the masses reached; and only when conscience is reached, when it kindles the fires of the heart, are things brought to that white heat of enthusiasm which consumes the *debris* of the past, and turns out the new coin of reform. Do kings, steadily retreating before the encroaching demands of the people, take refuge behind the doors of the Church, and claim the divine right of kings? Taught of God to uphold existing governments, and to respect its representatives, the Church will defend for a time the king and the doctrine. But when at length the eyes of the Church are opened to the fact that this man is not exercising his divine mission for its ordained purpose, but as a vantage point to indulge in personal vice and to tyrannize over the people; when she learns that the divine establishment does not mean the divine appointment of any special form of government, or protection for wicked governors; when the Church realizes these facts, and withdraws her protection from the royal culprit, his doom has always been sealed. Just so with every reform that has succeeded in establishing itself among men.

So it has been with the present social order, with the received customs of getting and holding property. The wealthy classes have naturally found in the Church a protector of the right of private property, both because it commends itself to the conservative judgment, and she finds it recognized in her Bible. But when the Church wakes up to realize how these wealthy classes are ignoring every obligation that rests upon them as such, that their wealth is not at all held as a trust, but as means to indulge themselves, that every condition which God has affixed to the title he gives is being violated, then it will become the duty of the Church and her ministry to speak in no uncertain sound on these great subjects.

1. The first duty of the Church in the present crisis is to study carefully these great principles involved in these questions, and especially to find out the teaching of the Bible on the subject, and then to fearlessly deliver the truth to men as God shall give her to see it. She should not be deterred by the opposition she will awaken on the one hand, nor should she be hurried into political alliances on the other. She should find out the truth and preach it.

2. She should insist upon her members putting in practice the principles of Christ in money matters as in all else. She should deliver a faithful gospel to

her rich members; she should show them what Christ requires of them. She should do all she can to awaken a sentiment in her own ranks in favor of the trusteeship of wealth, not as a theory but in practice; and condemning all misuse of the sacred trust God has committed to his wealthy children, she should lift her voice in condemnation of the sinful indulgence and the wasteful extravagance of the very rich. She should let all parties know that she has no defense for property that is obtained or held contrary to the law of God. She should teach the wicked rich that they cannot fall behind her bulwarks to fight socialism, and at the same time ignore every principle which she has been commissioned to preach. Let her say to them: "Accept the principles of the Bible as they relate to money matters, and embody those principles in your lives, and we will defend your private title to the last; but if you refuse this, then you must get from behind our fortifications, and fight the socialist out in the open field, and we will not lift a voice or a hand in your defense."

The Church must herself believe in her Master, must believe that he is wiser than all others in all ages, must believe that only his infinite mind can grasp the laws of sociology, must believe that whatever he has revealed is true, and that all his principles can and should be put in practice, and she should demand that we make experiment of them in practical life. It may have been impracticable in the past to have put some of these principles to the test, some may lie beyond our present development; but assuredly the world has reached the point where the Church should insist on trying the economic principles of his word, a point where the world needs and must have these principles put in actual practice, or she will seek for a different order. Christianity is on trial in this crisis as she has never been before. If her representatives let the world go elsewhere for the solution of the present problems than to Christ, it will be such a disparagement of the Master as has never before been given; and it will be a blow from which his cause will recover with difficulty. If, however, man can be persuaded to put the principles of Christ to a practical test, and they do, as if given a fair trial they will, solve our difficulties, then the peasant of Galilee shall be shown to be the son of God, the possessor of infinite wisdom.

3. The Church, while keeping in sympathy with the upper classes if she can, and while defending their real rights, must remember that her great mission is to the mass of mankind, to God's poor. In the Master's day the poor had the gospel preached unto them. Woe unto us if we cut the cord of sympathy between the poor and the cause of Christ. As the result of the natural conservatism of the Church leading her to a general defense of the right of private property, she has strained the love of many of the masses. She has been identified and denounced as the mere defender of the rich man. While still doing justice to the rich man, and still defending him so far as he is right, she must see to it that she does not sacrifice the law of Christ in her effort to fight the rich man's battles. And she must convince the poor man of her real interest in all that affects him and his house. She must show him her sympathy and extend her help. Never was there a time

when these two needed one another more than they do just now. Great will be the folly of either in antagonizing the other at such a time as this. They must stand and fall together.

4. In this great effort to lead to a right adjustment of economic principles and so help to solve the economic questions that are now distracting the public let not the Church suppose that her mission is accomplished when she establishes a few more charitable institutions or puts a few of her preachers to lecturing to the people on socialistic questions. Concerts, lectures, charitable institutions are well enough in their place, but the crisis that is now on us calls for something mightier than these; and that something is the teaching of Christ put into practice. Christ is the Saviour of the world, and he alone can save.

THE END.